LAUGHING TOGETHER

LAUGHING TOGETHER

Giggles and Grins from Around the Globe

Compiled by Barbara K. Walker
with Everybody Else's Help

Designed and Illustrated by Simms Taback

Free Spirit Publishing/Minneapolis
in cooperation with the U.S. Committee for UNICEF

Free Spirit
PUBLISHING

LIBRARY OF CONGRESS CATALOGING-IN-PUBLICATION DATA

Laughing Together : giggles and grins from around the globe / compiled by Barbara K. Walker with everybody else's help ; designed and illustrated by Simms Taback.
    p.   cm.
   Includes index.
   ISBN 0-915793-37-7
    1. Wit and humor, juvenile. 2. Wit and humor. 3. Jokes.
 I. Walker, Barbara K. II. Taback, Simms.
PN6153.L334 1992
808.88'2—dc20   91-43784
                                                 CIP
                                                 AC

10 9 8 7 6 5 4 3
Printed in the United States of America

Free Spirit Publishing Inc.
400 First Avenue North, Suite 616
Minneapolis, MN 55401
(612)338-2068

*Dedicated, with love,
to children everywhere*

Acknowledgments

Laughing Together is the result of the joyous contributions of people of all ages from all parts of the world. In these four pages you will find the names of many of those whose jokes or rhymes or riddles are used in the book and of some people whose "funnies" couldn't be included because of space limitations. Listed with the "jokers" are the translators who worked patiently to turn into English the flavor and fun of the jokes in other languages, not at all an easy job. In a separate listing, credit is given for printed and recorded sources quoted or adapted. Thanks, all of you, for sharing your laughter with us!

First, for help on the book from its very beginning, my special thanks go to Anne Pellowski, Director-Librarian of the Information Center on Children's Cultures, U.S. Committee for UNICEF; to Lavinia Dobler, of Scholastic Magazines, Inc.; to Ann Morgan and her staff, of the International Programs office at Texas Tech University; to Ann Miller, of Texas Tech University; to the staffs of the Lubbock City-County Libraries and the Texas Tech University Library; to Walter Scherf, Director of the International Youth Library in Munich; and to my husband, Dr. Warren S. Walker, who shares my deep concern for international understanding and appreciation.

Now, listed by countries or ethnic groups, are those others who helped with *Laughing Together*: Afghanistan—Joan Kayeum, John Walsh; Argentina— Rosanna De Bernardis, Alejandro Guzman-Stein; Australia—Gwenda Davey, Stephen H. Long, the students at Huntingdale Technical School in Melbourne; Austria—Erika Adams, Josef Finder, International Institute for Children's Literature and Reading Research; Bangladesh—Halide M. Salam; Bolivia— Luiz Jiminez; Botswana—Botsang Mosienyane; Brazil—Cremilda Toledo Lee, Tamira Quesada, Claudio de Souza; Bulgaria—Tanya V. Christensen, Alice Markoff; Burma—John Hpa, Stephen H. Long; Canada—Bertha Helen Kerr, students recruited by Alice Markoff from a French-language school in Toronto, neighbors in McGregor Bay, Ontario; Chile—Alicia Morel de Thayer; Chinese—Irene Cheng, Jean Sie Koh, Maria A. Pan; Costa Rica—Consular Service in Lubbock, Texas; Cuba— Lourdes Kuethe; Czechoslovakia—Stuart Amor, Nancy Fowler, Bohumil Hrubý, Z. K. Slabý, Věra Součkova; Denmark— P. Merville Larson; Ecuador—Patricia Burbano Pérez; Egypt—Malaka Finco, Huda Masseoud; Estonian— Terttu Hummasti; Ethiopia—Rita Pankhurst, Aranios W. Yohannes; Finland— Lee Andrews, Terttu Hummasti; France— Beatrice Alexander, Doan Nguyen, Geneviève Patte, Antoinette Sanger, Anthea Shackleton; Germany—Christian Kloesel, Wilfred Wiegand, Ann Wood; Ghana—Joshua Owusu; Greece—Constantine Karmokolias; Guyana Thakoor Persaud; Hong Kong—Minnie Chang, L. S. Chen, Maggie Chui; Hungary— Michály Simai; India—Suniti Ponkshe, K. Ramakrishnan; Indonesia—Michael Tjahjadi, Tinco E. A. van Hylckama; Iran—Ali Reza Amir-Moéz, Djafar Badi'i; Ireland—Bridget O'Farrell Ray; Israel—Ramzi Said Baransi, Lorraine Cohen, Lana Kay Evans, Greta Golden, Bernice Zibilich; Italy—Carla Poesio, Mina Stewart; Jamaica—Gerald Uhlfelder; Japan—Hirokazu Haga, Shonosuke Kanehira, Shuji Usugi; Kenya—Joseph K. Kibera; Korea—Won-Ja Bae Park, Young Pil Park, Young-Ja Shin Yough; Kuwait—Abdul-Salam A. Anshasi; Laos—James W. Roginski; Latvian—Leonid A. Jirgensons; Lebanon—Boutros El-Sabaaly; Lesotho—Reatile S. Mochebelele, Edwin Seitlheko; Liberia— A. Doris Banks Henries; Madagascar—Nicole Koplin; Malaysia—Paul W. Juby, Horace F. Mathis; Malta—Tito Sammut; Mexico—Mauricio Charpenel, Jason O. Rodríguez, Bea Strehli; Morocco—Harold Berson; Netherlands—Tinco E. A. van Hylckama, Francien Wright; Netherlands Antilles—Francien Wright; Nicaragua—Angela McEwan; Nigeria—Adeyola David; Norway—Aud Bohn Kristiansen; Pakistan—Saeed M. Ismail, Muhammad Latif; Panama—Monica Cheryl Hall; Peru—Rosanna De Bernardis, Ralph Bolton, Victor Leon-Rocca; Philippines—Herminia Q. Meñez, Grace Smith, Jasmin T. Woodhouse; Poland—Krystyna Baker; Portugal—Tamira Quesada; Saudi Arabia—Abdul-Hamid J. Al-Tayyib, Saleh A. Omair; Scotland—Robert Wilson; Sierra Leone —Verna Aardema Vugteveen (for "How Spider Sold a Big 'Dog' "); Singapore— Ng Kim Beng; South Africa—June Fair, Johanna Muller; Spain—Margarita Soteras; Sri Lanka—Eric Ranawake; Swaziland—Brenton Bonsani Xaba; Switzerland—Ursula Straub; Syria—Amer Satli; Thailand—Narong R. Indachandr, S. Rujikietqumjorn; Turkey—Archive of Turkish Oral Narrative, Neriman Güven, Neriman Hizir, Reyhan Senol, Metin Tamkoç; U.S.S.R.— Krystyna Baker; U.S.A.—Lana Kay Evans, Eleanor Kline, Helen Scannell,

the students of Maedgen Elementary School, Lubbock, Texas; Venezuela—
Angela McEwan; Vietnam—Doan Nguyen; Yugoslavia—Peter D. Bubresko,
Ivan Kušan, Miroslav Rodič; Zaïre—Mabel Ross.

Thanks are gratefully rendered to the publishers for permission to use the
following printed or recorded sources for reproduction or translation or
adaptation: "Afghan Riddles," by Joan Kayeum (dittoed article); *Alors
Raconte . . .* , by François Biron and Georges Folgoas (Paris: Éditions Mengès,
1976); *Biba Nanzi!*, by J. Droog (Aruba, Netherlands Antilles: Serie Volksverhal-
en, [no date]); *Big Merry Discourses and Tales*, by Ran Vosilek (Sophia, 1974);
Cinderella Dressed in Yella, by Ian Turner, editor (Melbourne: Heinemann,
1969); *The Counting-Out Rhymes of Children: Their Antiquity, Origin, and
Wide Distribution*, by Henry Carrington Bolton (New York: D. Appleton, 1888;
reissued Detroit: Singing Tree Press, Book Tower, 1969); *Laos Folk-Lore of
Farther India*, by Katherine N. Fleeson (New York: Fleming H. Revell, 1899);
El libro de oro de los niños, Vol. II, by Benjamin Barnes (Mexico: Acropolis,
1946); *The Lore and Language of Schoolchildren,* by Iona and Peter Opie
(London: Oxford University Press, 1959) © Iona and Peter Opie, 1959, by
permission of the Oxford University Press; *Mafalda*, by Quino (Buenos Aires:
Ediciones de La Flor, 1971); *Poems by Children: 1950–1961,* edited by
M. Baldwin (London: Routledge & Kegan Paul); *Pun and Fuzzles!,*
by Audrey and Dodie McKim (Richmond Hill, Ontario: Scholastic-TAB
Publications, 1974); *Scandinavian Roundabout*, by Agnes Rothery (New York:
Dodd, Mead, 1952); *Small Sabra Anecdotes—666 Jokes for Children*, compiled
and edited by A. Gad (Tel Aviv: Joseph Sreberk Ltd., 1973); *Spoken Finnish,*
by Thomas A. Sebeok (New York: Holt, 1947); *A Treasury of Mexican
Folkways*, by Frances Toor (New York: Crown, 1947) copyright 1947, 1975
by Crown Publishers, Inc., used by permission of Crown Publishers, Inc.;
Wit and Wisdom of West Africa, by Richard R. Burton (London: Tinsley,
1865); *Allers* (a family magazine published in Norway); *The Asian Student*
(a newspaper published in San Francisco by The Asia Foundation); *Aurora*
(the magazine of Queen's College, Lagos, Nigeria) *Bikhan Wa Bidan* (a
children's magazine published in Afghanistan); *The Black Market Book of
Jokes* (a booklet compiled by the students of Huntingdale Technical School,
Melbourne, Australia); *Bulgarche* (a Bulgarian family magazine); *China Daily*
(a newspaper published in Taiwan); *Corriere dei Ragazzi* (an Italian children's
magazine); *The Daily Gleaner* (a newspaper published in Kingston, Jamaica);
Elizabethan (a children's magazine published in England); *Fugulha* (a

children's magazine published in Portugal); *Funny Cartoons* (a children's magazine published in the U.S.S.R.); *Il Giornalino* (a children's magazine published in Italy); *Jewish Daily Forward* (a newspaper published in the United States); *Joker* (an activities magazine for children published in France, but distributed also in Belgium, Canada, Martinique, and Switzerland); *Junge Schar* (a children's magazine published in West Germany); *Junior Mirror* (a children's newspaper published in England); *Kayhan-e-Bacheha* (an Iranian children's magazine); *Little Blue Stockings* (a school magazine published in Manila, Philippines); *Le Matin* (a newspaper published in Casablanca, Morocco); *Mônica* (a children's magazine published in Brazil); *Murzinka* (a Boy Scout magazine published in the U.S.S.R.), *El Nacional* (a newspaper published in Venezuela); *Ohníček* (a Czechoslovakian children's magazine); *Orbit* (a children's magazine published in Zambia); *Paik Daneshamooz* and *Paik Daneshamooz va Paik Moálem* (Iranian children's magazines for use in the schools); *Peter and the World* (unpublished manuscript of anecdotes by Z. K. Slabý); *El Plata* (a newspaper published in Uruguay), *Read* (the magazine of the Sierra Leone Library Board); *Sesinho* (a Brazilian children's magazine); *Si-Kuntjung* (an Indonesian children's magazine); *Smilje i Bosilje* [*SMIB*] (a Yugoslavian children's magazine); *Soviet Life* (a magazine published in Moscow and also in Washington, D.C.); *Students' Digest* (a newspaper published in New Zealand for young people); *Sunshine* (a children's magazine published in Poona, India); *Teen and Twenty: Africa's Youth Magazine* (a magazine by and for young people published in Lagos, Nigeria); *Tricolor* (a children's magazine published in Venezuela); *Venture* (a magazine for young men published in the United States); *La Vie Catholique* (a family magazine published in France but widely circulated elsewhere); *El Volantín* (a children's magazine in Chile circulated among employees in a metal company); *Ten Spanish-Language Songs for Children of All Ages*, sung by Jenny Wells Vincent (Amerecord ALP-102; Taos, New Mexico: Cantemos Records, [no date]); a tape cassette of jokes told by students at Huntingdale Technical School, Melbourne (Melbourne: Gwenda Davey, 1976).

If I have overlooked anyone or any publication furnishing help in the compiling of *Laughing Together*, it has not been an intentional oversight. No one knows better than I that a book filled from cover to cover with fun would *have* to be the work of many hands and heads and hearts and senses of humor. Together, I trust that we have pleased the world's children as much as their laughter pleases us.

Contents

▲▲▲▲▲▲▲▲▲▲▲▲▲▲▲▲▲▲▲

▼▼▼▼▼▼▼▼▼▼▼▼▼▼▼▼▼▼▼

Foreword

Many comedians have confessed that the hardest work on earth is making people laugh. The world itself is serious; the people around the world have more problems than they can handle. People seem to have neither the time nor the heart to laugh. Yet of all the acts of which human beings are capable, laughing is probably the most essential to survival and sanity.

Where can we turn for honest-to-goodness laughter? Who knows how to laugh without hurting anybody else? Who doesn't need politics or national differences or racial contrasts or any other friction-producing ingredients in order to make good jokes? Children are the ones who can meet this world hunger for humor: eager, open, full of fun, and *curious* about differences but not *critical* of those differences. *Laughing Together* is a gift from the world's children, a **UNICEF** package to meet the most basic kind of need we can name, the need for rediscovering how to laugh together and thus to live together.

Increasingly, we have become aware of walls—walls between one nation and another, one political system and another, one religion and another, one race and another, even between one sex and another. Something must put windows in those walls, something which requires neither a visa nor a passport, something which is not barred by language differences, something which is truly universal. That "something" is laughter, but not just *anybody*'s laughter: it is the laughter of children, shared through jokes that have a common base in the ability of children to stand back and see the important things, undismayed by outward differences and disputes.

In fact, children's laughter is itself a language, a truly international language. It is through the language of children's laughter that we can come to understand two great truths: (1) The world's peoples have more in common than they have in conflict; this fact draws us together. (2) The differences among peoples give them special flavors; these make us interesting to each other.

The jokes, cartoons, riddles, rhymes, and short tales chosen for this book represent both the universal base and the individual differences that can enable us to live together in peace. They are drawn from all six continents (Oceania and New Zealand have been grouped with Australia) and sample the humor of nearly one hundred countries, political groups, or ethnic groups; for some of these groups (e.g. Chinese, Estonian) we have selected jokes from among those living in the United States and Canada, as well as from the homeland. As often as possible, the jokes appear in their original languages as well as in English. The basic content of the jokes is worldwide in interest and concern; the details in the jokes—names, units of money, foods, vegetation, and animals—and the languages used mark the local differences that fit any particular joke for its own culture.

English has been used as the translation language, but surely the inclusion of samples of all the original languages tempts readers to experiment with languages other than their own, to discover both similarities and differences, and to rediscover the importance and dignity of having a language especially suited to its own culture.

The jokes in *Laughing Together* are hearty, innocent of malice and meanness, reflecting primary human concerns—food, clothing, shelter, fear, curiosity, self-centeredness, need for approval—and truly funny to the children among whom they are told. Not all of these jokes will be funny to all readers. On the other hand, many of the jokes will prompt this response: "I know one something like that, only *mine* goes *this* way. . . ."

If we can laugh together, we can learn to live together. And I am confident that we *can* laugh together if we can stand still long enough to listen to children, who see to the heart and speak from the heart.

Barbara K. Walker

A Special Note
for Teachers and Parents

Today's children, whether at school, at home, or at play, carry a burden of concerns far too heavy and complex to handle without that special tool called humor. By beginning with the international children's jokes in *Laughing Together: Giggles and Grins from Around the Globe*, you can help the young people in your care to discover that children *everywhere* face the same kinds of concerns: world unrest, parent-child confrontations, sibling rivalries, school skirmishes, hunger, self-consciousness, unfulfilled wishes. You can share their joy in finding that kids their age but far, far away are coping with many of these same concerns by telling jokes surprisingly like the ones they themselves use to "take the heat off."

These jokes, then, can be a launching pad toward developing the coping tool of humor, which more often than not evidences itself in laughter. Laughter, not just at jokes being told, but also at ridiculous occurrences on school, family, and playground fronts, is—as musical comedian Victor Borge once said—"the shortest distance between two people," whether teacher and student, parent and child, or one kid and another. Laughter is especially needed by children who are gifted and those who are learning different (LD), whether grouped or main-streamed, because of all school-age youngsters they tend to feel most "labeled" and thus most lonely. So identified, they experience appreciable stress. Response to that stress ranges from seeming cockiness to apparent boredom to demoralized underachievement. The young person who laughs when reprimanded by an authority figure—teacher, principal, parent—is not laughing out of joy or scorn or impertinence but, more often than not, out of nervousness and anxiety. Yes, the laughter itself is risky: it may produce disbelief and outrage in the authority figure, and demeaning comments may follow. But risk is part of growing, inside and out. Even a turtle has to stick its neck out in order to get ahead.

There is *good* laughter, wholesome laughter, that springs from a developing sense of humor. This can protect all young people from debilitating stress. It can help you as teachers, parents, and counselors to live responsibly and happily with the exciting challenges all kids bring to their encounters with adults and with each other. Laughter is tonic for both mind and body: it expands the lungs, stimulates circulation, clears the brain for thinking, and even improves digestion. It is safe to say that a teacher or parent who has not laughed with a child or children can count that day lost for growth and learning, for laughter relieves tension for everyone and thus creates a climate encouraging to shared learning.

Laughing Together widens the lens of humor to capture jokes and anecdotes from children worldwide. Ideally, each child and adult would have a copy of the book to use. Since this is not an ideal world, a copy for each group of four or five children would provide them and their teacher and parent with sufficient ammunition to expand both their stock of jokes and their understanding of many cultures other than their own.

As a starter for your own ideas of ways to use the book as a bonding agent at school or at home, try some or all of the approaches suggested on the following pages. If you find others that work particularly well for you, I'd appreciate knowing about them so that they can be included (and appropriately credited!) in a subsequent printing of this international children's joke book. Suggestions can be sent to me at the following address:

Barbara K. Walker
c/o Free Spirit Publishing Inc.
400 First Avenue North, Suite 616
Minneapolis, MN 55401

Thanks!

The Tip of an Iceberg of Ideas

1. Try a Scrambler game.
You will need copies of *Laughing Together*, a world map or globe, and several eager lookers. As the source of each joke is identified, locate the country and continent on the map. Then ask questions such as the following:

a. In which countries in *Laughing Together* can you find jokes or riddles about birds or fowl? (TIP: There are 15 countries.)

b. In which countries in *Laughing Together* can you find jokes about eating or about food (except eggs!)? (TIP: There are 37 countries.)

c. In which countries in *Laughing Together* can you find jokes in which kids play tricks on teachers? (TIP: There are 20 countries.)

d. In which countries in *Laughing Together* can you find jokes in which kids play tricks on parents/grandparents? (TIP: There are 15 countries.)

2. Try role-playing.
Divide the group into pairs.

a. Role-play the joke from Peru on page 38. Then invent and role-play a joke using a similar setting and trick from your own country or culture.

b. Role-play the centipede joke from Germany on page 62, using two students who are studying German to play the roles in German.

c. Role-play the Czechoslovakian joke on page 44. Then invent and role-play a joke of your own explaining why you were late getting home from your school. (Provide as nonsensical an excuse as you can imagine!)

d. Role-play the joke from Ghana on page 55, doing the best you can to represent the "Twi" sounds (substitute "Father" or "Mother" for "Family"). Then find Ghana on the map. Do tribal language differences explain to some degree why peace is so hard to maintain in newly developing African democracies?

3. Meet these challenges.

a. Have a volunteer read aloud the short folk tale from Sierra Leone on page 63. Then choose two students to go to the library, find collections of Anansi (Spider) stories from West Africa, and take turns reading aloud two or three Anansi tales. Is Spider limited to West Africa? (See pages 67-70 in *Laughing Together*.) How do you think Spider got to Aruba from West Africa? Where else can Spider tales be found? How did they travel?

b. Find five jokes or drawings in *Laughing Together* that would not seem funny to most English-speaking kids because of a word or words peculiar to that non-English-speaking culture. Locate on a map or globe the five countries represented. To *some* English-speaking children, those same puzzling jokes *would* seem funny. What factor makes those few kids able to appreciate those jokes or drawings?

c. Locate six jokes in *Laughing Together* that include coins strange to most English-speaking people. Find the current values of those coins in terms of your own country's coins.

d. Parodies of some common English/American poems can be found in *Laughing Together*. Locate the parodies, provide a common "original" verse for each one, and then create your own parody for one verse.

e. Limericks are a worldwide favorite of children. In *Laughing Together*, find three limericks, locate their respective countries of origin, and then provide three limericks of your own that are appropriate for settings in three non-English-speaking cultures. (Use clues in *Laughing Together* to supply appropriate foods, coins, names, or situations.)

f. Tongue-twisters, or tongue-tanglers, are found among children in most cultures. Choose the non-English tongue-twister in *Laughing Together* that seems most tricky and fun in its *original* form, and identify its language or dialect and country of origin. Then, using the international phonetic alphabet, practice that tongue-twister until you can teach it to someone else in your class or your family. Also, if the original form uses special characters (such as the Korean tongue-twister on page 97), see how close you can come to writing the characters as they appear in *Laughing Together*.

g. Invite to your class or home someone whose native language provided a joke, a tongue-twister, or a counting-out rhyme for *Laughing Together*. Find out how to pronounce the words correctly. Also, learn some new and special things about the country from which that language comes.

4. Try this ongoing project.

Begin your own joke journal, writing down each day at least one joke that will give you the lift you need on a day when nothing at all seems funny. Such a journal is a wonderful safety valve. You'll be amazed at how many really "down" events can be viewed as "up" events just a few days or a few weeks later. What's more, you'll be well on your way to developing a sound sense of humor that will ease your relationships with everybody else and with yourself, too. Remember: Those who laugh, last!

I hope you have as much fun with this book and with the people you meet in it as I did!

Dlaczego?

WHY?

Dlaczego żuraw podnosi jedną nogę stojąc nad wodą?
Dlatego, że gdyby podniósl jeszcze drugą nogę, toby upadl na ziemię.

Why does a crane raise one leg when he stands in the water?
Because if he raised the other leg, he would fall down.

(from Poland)

LAUGHING TOGETHER

Family Funnies

"Nobody—but *nobody*—has a family as crazy (or nice, or naggy, or selfish) as mine!" Have you ever heard yourself saying these words? Or thinking them? Well, come join the club!

On all six continents, family members tease and trick and love each other, with the oldest, tallest, strongest ones just as often on the losing end as the "two-bit critters" they are trying to lick into shape. The one thing all these families have in abundance is laughter, the grease that keeps the wheels from squeaking in this "feeling machine" that is the family.

Need proof? This chapter opens windows on families in thirty-nine different countries, in fifteen languages besides English. What can we see through these windows? Juan Tamad's mother in the Philippines and Ikpehare's mother in Nigeria nag about eating habits (just as yours does), with funny but quite different results. Mom teases Dad in Switzerland, in Nigeria—you name it! And brothers and sisters squabble and tease and pretend to share from one curve of the earth to the other. Baby brothers and sisters are universally viewed with mild disapproval, though they have their good points as they grow old enough to turn the tables on their elders. (By the way, did you ever hear of a "brother" sandwich?)

The "home" end of home-and-school is a real eye-opener. Yes, there really are jokes about signing report cards in the dark, not only in Mexico but in Iran, Hong Kong, France, the United States, and elsewhere. And the long arms of the teacher and the principal tilt many a dinner-table conversation...

When your dad walks in his sleep, does he go off with the igloo? When he snores, is his nose "awake"? Would you like to keep house inside a lion? Try it; you might like it...Macarena did!

GREECE

Ἡ δασκάλα τοῦ Γιαννάκη τηλεϐώνησε στὴν μητέρα του ὅτι σήμερα ἦταν ἄτακτος. Ὅταν αὐτός ἔϐθασε ὀτό σπίτι, ἡ μητέρα του τόν ρώτησε ἂη ἦταν ϐρόνιμος.

— Ναί, ἀπήντησε αὐτός.

— Πρόϐεχε Γιαννάκη, τοῦ εἶπτ. Εἶναι κακό νὰ λὲς ψέμματα. Κάποιο πουλάκι μοὺ εἶπε ὅτι ἤϐουν ἄτακτος !

Καί ὁ Γιαννάκης κουνώντας τό κεϐὰλ !

— Πρόσεχε μαμά, τὰ πουλάκια δὲν μιλᾶνε !

Yiannakis's teacher called his mother and told her that he was disobedient. When he came home his mother asked him whether he had behaved well at school.

"Yes," he replied.

"Watch out," she said. "It's a bad thing to lie. A little bird told me that you were disobedient!"

"Watch out, Mom. Birds can't talk!"

ROMANIA

Mother: Ileana, what do you have for your homework tonight?

Ileana: Nothing, Mother— except watch TV!

BELGIUM

Someone asked: Well, Jean-Claude, what do you think of your new baby brother?

Jean-Claude: If you want to know, there are a lot of things we needed more around this house!

NIGERIA

Mother: Now, Kofi, don't be selfish. Let your little brother share the bicycle with you.

Kofi: But Mother, I do. I ride it down the hill, and he rides it up the hill.

VENEZUELA

Juanita: Mama, why did Papa put that great big fat bandage on the head of his hammer?

Mama: Well, the first time he tried to put up a nail for hanging your diploma, he hit his thumb and then the wall. *This* time, he says he'll hurt only the nail!

SCOTLAND

Little Brother: I know what you're going to say next.

Big Brother: What?

Little Brother: See? I *knew* you'd say "What?"!

IRAN

A Kind Brother

Mother: Jamshid, this swing belongs to you and your brother. You must share it with him.

Jamshid: We always share it. I sit in the swing, and he pushes me.

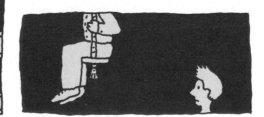

PHILIPPINES

The family was gathered at dinner. Juan Tamad quickly finished his meal and got up, preparing to leave. His mother, disturbed by Juan's behavior, called him back. "Juan! When there are others still eating, it is not polite to get up and leave the table. Try to remember, and don't ever do it again."

The next day, Juan Tamad was sent to the marketplace to buy a *ganta* of rice. On his way, he stopped at a snack bar to buy his favorite treat, a rice cake.

Nighttime came, and Juan Tamad's family had become very worried. It was only a short distance to the market, and Juan had been gone all day. Finally Juan's mother sent his father to go after him and find out what had happened.

His father went to the market and found Juan Tamad still sitting at the snack bar. "What are you doing here?" he asked.

Juan Tamad answered, "I'm waiting for the people to finish eating. Mother said it's not polite to leave while others are eating. I've been sitting here all day waiting for everybody to finish so I can go!"

Note: Juan Tamad, or "Lazy John," is a popular subject for jokes and tales in the Philippines. The original story was told in Tagalog, a dialect of Filipino, the national language. Here, as in many jokes, Juan Tamad is not too bright.

BULGARIA

A father said to his sons:

"Tomorrow your mother is going to bake a pie. Who is going to eat it?"
The oldest son replied:

"Father, I'll eat it all!"
The father then said:

"Tomorrow I am going to butcher a pig. Who is going to eat it?"
The same son answered:

"Father, I'll eat it all!"
The father added:

"Tomorrow we are going to plow the field. Who is going to plow?"
The oldest son answered again:

"It's always me, always me. Now it's somebody else's turn to volunteer."

CHILE

The Fur House

Once upon a time, many years ago, there was a little girl named Macarena who used to live in a house. Her friends called her Maca.

When Macarena was five years old she started in school and she was very studious, but one day she got lazy and she only made *three*'s on her report card.

Well, when Macarena went home, suddenly a lion ate her up. Her mother started to cry when she found out Macarena had been eaten by a lion, and she decided to look for the lion, and the lion ate her up too. After eating up the mother, the lion went close to the house because he wanted to eat up her brother Andrés and her father. When Andrés came out of the house and saw the lion, he started to run away, but it was too late because the lion caught up with him and ate him up. The poor father went to look for his son, without noticing that the lion was following him, and the lion pounced on him and ate up the father. And this is the way they lived very happily in the stomach of the lion and they weren't sad anymore because they were together.

Maria Teresa Aubert
Nine years old

GREECE

Little Petrakis was afraid to play in the backyard because he thought he was corn and he was afraid that the chickens might eat him. After a great deal of effort, his mother convinced him that he was not corn, and so the next day Petrakis went out to the yard. But before too long, he rushed in again, scared.

"What happened?" his mother asked.

"Well, there are chickens out there," he said.

"So what? You know you are not corn!"

"Well, *I* do. But do the chickens know it, too?"

NORWAY

Unanok, ... du går i søvne igjen!

———

"Unanok, ... you're walking in your sleep again!"

URUGUAY

—Abuelita, ¿tus gafas son de aumento?

—Si, hijo.

—Entonces, quitatelas para cortame el pastel.

———

"Grandma, are your glasses the kind that make things bigger?"

"Yes, son."

"Then take them off and use them to cut a piece of cake for me."

COSTA RICA

Mother: Why is your brother Paco crying? Did he fail his exam?

Felipe: No. His best paper boat sailed into the sewer!

CZECHOSLOVAKIA

A gentleman walking across a bridge sees a small boy looking over the railing and crying. Being a good-natured fellow, he stops and says, "Why are you crying?"

The boy answers, with his eyes full of tears, "My sandwich fell in the water."

"What? You lost a sandwich? That's not so bad that you need to cry about it."

"Yes, but . . ." The boy, still crying, tries to explain his trouble.

"Hmnn," said the gentleman, still puzzled. "That must have been an especially good sandwich. Was it with cheese?"

"No, Sir."

"Was it with sausage?"

"No, Sir."

"Tell me, What was it with, then?"

"My brother!"

WALES

Taid a nain yn rhedeg râs.
I fyny'r ffordd fain ac at y plâs,
Syrthiodd nain ar draws y stôl,
Ha! Ha! ebe taid, Mae nain ar ôl.

———————

Grandfather and grandmother
    running a race,
Up the narrow road and to the
    big place (house);
Grandma fell over a stool
    (how blind . . .);
"Ha! Ha!" cried Grandpa;
    "She's fallen behind."

Note: A somewhat free translation to retain the rhyme and the spirit of the Welsh.

CHINESE

It was raining outdoors. Four-year-old Shou-Lei was crying as if her heart would break. Her mother said to the servant girl, "Just a few minutes ago I saw her playing very happily in the garden. Why has she suddenly become so sad?"

The servant girl answered, "Yes, Ma'am. She was playing very happily with her marbles in a hole I dug in the ground for her. But now that it's raining, she wants me to move the hole into the house."

———————

屋外下著大雨，四歲的小麗則在屋子裡哭得很大聲。她媽媽就問
女嫗説：「剛才我見她在後院玩得很開心，為什麽她忽然間會哭得這麽厲害？」
女嫗道：「剛才她玩得很開心是因為我替她在地上控了一個小洞洞讓她玩弹珠。」
小麗媽又問：「可是…」
女嫗道：「可是，現在她卻要我把小洞洞搬到屋子裡來。」

(Note: Usually, Chinese is written in columns, starting from the upper right and reading down the first column to the bottom, then moving left to the second column, and so on. [For an example, see "Watermelon Rind," on page 91.] This particular joke has been rewritten in Chinese in "English" style.)

PAKISTAN

Grandfather: Well, Habib, how is your position at school?

Habib: Very fine, Grandfather—center forward in soccer and right back in studies.

HA
HA
HA
HA
HA
HA
HA
HA
HA
HA
HA

U.S.A.

Mother: Dad and I asked you *not* to paste pictures on your new wall!

Brian: Oh, but these'll come down easily, Mom. I stuck them up with peanut butter. . . .

SOUTH AFRICA

When Pietie was four years of age his snobbish parents, who decided he wasn't attentive enough for his age, sent him to a psychiatrist in order to find out whether anything could be done about his inattentiveness.

Doctor: Pietie, how many ears has a cat?

Pietie: Two.

Doctor: How many legs has a cat?

Pietie: Four.

Doctor: How many eyes has a cat?

Pietie: Two.

Doctor: And how many tails has a cat?

Pietie: My goodness, doctor, haven't you ever seen a cat before?

HO HO HO HO HO HO HO HO HO HO HO HO HO HO HO HO HO HO HO HO HO HO HO

VENEZUELA

—Nena, ahora que vas a la escuela dime ¿de dónde sacan el algodón?

—¡Papá! De donde va a ser . . . de la almohada.

———

Nena, now that you are going to school, tell me, "Where does cotton come from?"

Papa! It comes from . . . from the cushion.

BULGARIA

Mother: What on earth are you doing with a full-grown elephant in our little apartment?

Son: It's O.K. I'm only keeping it overnight!

ISRAEL

Note: Hebrew, like a number of other languages, is read from right to left.

עוֹדֵד חוֹזֵר הַבַּיְתָה רָטֹב מְאֹד.
הָאֵם: הֵיכָן נִרְטַבְתָּ כָּל־כָּךְ ?
עוֹדֵד: פָּגַשְׁתִּי בְּרֵז־מַיִם...

Oded returns home very wet.

Mother: How come you got so wet?

Oded: I met a water faucet. . . .

FINLAND

Pekka: Anna minun olla rauhassa. Kirjoitan siskolleni.
Matti: Miksi kirjoitat niin hitaasti?
Pekka: Hän ei ossa lukea nopeasti.

———

Pekka: Leave me alone. I'm writing to my sister.

Matti: Why are you writing so slowly?

Pekka: She doesn't know how to read fast.

U.S.A.

George: Mama, when did you say my new baby brother was coming?

Mama: In just three weeks, dear! Mama will go to the hospital, and . . .

George: But, Mama, I've changed my mind. I've decided I'd rather have a dog!

TURKEY

Mehmet: Mother, could I please have a lira to give to that poor man shouting in the street?

Mother: Of course, my son. It's always good to give to the poor. But what is he shouting?

Mehmet: "Simi-i-i-ts! Two for one lira."

BURMA

Maung Lay was showing off his new skills in mathematics to his brother, who then said, "We'll see how clever you are. Listen very carefully to this simple problem: If a train traveling from Rangoon to Mandalay had 24 passengers, and when it reached Pegu 12 got off and 8 boarded, if in Taungoo 3 got off and 6 boarded, if in Meiktila 18 got off and 10 boarded, and if at the next stop 6 got off and 2 boarded, how many . . ."

"I know!" said Maung Lay. "I've been keeping count all the time!"

"All right, then," said his brother. "Tell me how many times the train stopped between Rangoon and Mandalay!"

MARTINIQUE

Mama: Do you want a cookie, Pierre? (Since there was no answer from her little son, she asked again.)
Mama: Pierre, do you want a cookie? Why must I ask you twice?
Pierre: Because I want two cookies!

VIETNAM

Bà nội nói với cháu bé: —nếu cháu hôn bà một cái nỏi má thì bà sẽ cho cháu một cây kẹo.
—Cháu phải hôn bà mấy cái thì mới được bà cho cả hộp kẹo?

Grandma: If you kiss me on my cheek one time, I'll give you a piece of candy.
Grandchild: How many kisses will it take for you to give me the whole box of candy?

MEXICO

A musician visiting the family had played several pieces on the piano: one for the father, another for the mother, a third for the grandmother and a fourth for the uncle. Finally, he asked the child of the household: "And you, little Juan, what piece do you prefer?"

Juan (half asleep because of the concert): "Me? A piece of chocolate!"

AUSTRIA

Little Mary goes to the confectioner's and asks, "How much is a plate of chocolate?"

"Ah, since it's you, one kiss," laughs the candy-maker.

"Oh, fine. Give me ten," says little Mary. "Grandma will pay you tomorrow."

CANADA

Big Brother: Bet you can't name one important thing we didn't have ten years ago.

Little Brother: I can, too—me!

JORDAN

Ahmad: Mother, I got one-hundred in two subjects.

Mother: Fine, Ahmad. What were they?

Ahmad: Forty in history and sixty in arithmetic.

INDONESIA

Anak: Mama, here is your money.

Ibu: Very honest, my child! Where did you get this money?

Anak: From your purse, Mama.

Ibu: ?????

POLAND

A little boy was running in the park and lost his mother. After a while, he approached a policeman and asked, "Sir, did you happen to see a lady without a boy like me?"

NIGERIA

A man quarreled with his wife and they decided not to speak to each other. The following day he returned from work to find that the meal was not ready. Before retiring to rest he left his wife a note which said, "Madam, wake me up when dinner is ready."

When dinner was ready the wife similarly left him a note on a table near his bed. In this note she wrote, "Master, awake, for dinner is now ready."

Bendy Nimsu
Form IVP

CANADA

Mother: Why did you put a spider in your sister's bed?

Mike: Because I couldn't find a snake.

U.S.A.

Visitor: George, what's the name of your new baby sister?

George: I don't know. I can't understand a word she says!

ISRAEL

Read from right to left

سأل طفل والده كي يشتري له طبل

الوالد : أخشى أن تزعجني به

الطفل : لا تخاف أستعمله فقط وأنت نائم

A child asked his father to get him a drum.

Father: I'm afraid that you will disturb me.

Child: No, Father. I'll just use it while you are sleeping.

U.S.A.

Hasten, Jason.
Bring the basin!
Whoops! Too late . . .
Bring the mop.

CZECHOSLOVAKIA

"Péto, běž podívat, jestli tatínek už spí." Péta se vrátí.
"Spí úplně celý. Jenom nos mu ještě neusnul."

———————

"Pete, go and look to see if Daddy is already asleep."

Peter comes back.

"All of Daddy is asleep except his nose."

IRAN

Ahmed: Is it true that some people can predict the future by looking at books?

Abdel: Indeed so. Whenever my mother looks at my books, she can tell what will happen to me by the end of the year!

MEXICO

—Papá, ¿puedes escribir en la
   oscuridad?
—Yo creo que sí, aunque no muy
   bien.
—Entonces, apaga la luz y firma mi
   boleta de calificaciones.

———

"Papa, can you write in the
   dark?"
"Yes, I think so, though not
   too well."
"Then you had better turn
   the light off and sign my
   report card."

KOREA

나도 적어 놓았시!

종이: "엄마, 아침 6시에 깨워
      달라고 색상 위에 작어 놓
      았는데 왜 안 깨웠어요?"
엄마: "그래서 나도 6시에 일어
      나라고 거기에 적어 놓았단
      다"

———

I Left a Note, Too!

Soong: Mom, why didn't you
   wake me up? I had left a
   note on the desk to wake me
   up at six in the morning.
Mother: I left a note there,
   too, to tell you to get up at six.

BELGIUM

It is Pierre's birthday, and his parents have taken him to a fine
   restaurant and told him he can have everything he wants to eat
   —and *only* what he wants to eat.
Waitress (after taking his parents' orders): And now, young man,
   what do you want?
Pierre: I'll begin and continue and end, Miss, with the desserts!

LATVIAN

Little Johnny was immersed in a book about the North Pole. Then, putting the book aside he gazed into the distance with a dreamy look.

"What are you thinking about, Johnny?" asked his mother.

"I wish we were living at the North Pole."

Mother, in surprise, "But it is very cold there."

"That's just it. Imagine how many times I wouldn't have to go to school because of the cold!"

———————

Mazais Jānītis aizrautīgi lasa grāmatu par ziemelpolu. Tad noliek grāmatu un sapnaini raugās tālumā.

"Par ko tu domā, Jānīti?"—

jautā māte.

"Es vēlētos, ka

mēs dzīvotu ziemelpolā."

"Tur taču loti auksts laiks," brīnās māte.

"Taisni tāpēc. Iedomājies tik, cik bieži tur aukstuma dēl nav jāiet skolā!"

HA HA HEE HO HA HA HA HEE HO HO HO HO HEE HEE HA HA HA HA HO HEE

SWITZERLAND

Hans: I should never have told my wife that I was hungry as a horse!

Karl: Why?

Hans: She brought me a pitchfork full of hay for dinner.

U.S.A.

Mom: You mean you fell over fifty feet and didn't even get hurt?

Tom: Yes. I was walking to the back of the school bus!

KUWAIT

There was a party in Jaber's house. Little Jaber asked his mother if he could eat with the guests. But his mother said, "You are too small. When your beard and moustache grow, then you can eat with us."

Little Jaber went to the small table which his mother set for him. Just as he started eating, a cat came to him. Jaber said crossly, "Hey, you cat! You have a beard and a moustache. Why don't you go to the guests' table and eat with them, and not come around to bother *me?*"

NIGERIA

Mother: Ikpehare, eat all your cereal so you will be big and strong like your daddy.

Ikpehare: All right, I'll eat it. But after it has made me big and strong, *nobody* is going to make me eat it!

AUSTRALIA

Mum: Eat your cabbage. It'll put colour in your cheeks.

Son: Who wants green cheeks?

CANADA

Mother: Pierre, what are you doing out here in the doghouse?

Pierre: Mother, when you're doing your spring cleaning, this is the only safe place to be!

ISRAEL

Ilan: Father, is the Messiah coming soon?

Father: Why do you want to know?

Ilan: I asked Deborah when we are going to have TV in the kibbutz, and she told me, "When the Messiah comes!"

U.S.A.

U.S.A.

Two brothers are riding their tandem bicycle along a narrow trail in Bear Mountain Park in New York.

Younger Brother: You're riding so close to the edge of the ravine that I'm getting dizzy!

Older Brother: Don't be so chicken! Close your eyes. That's what *I'm* doing.

U.S.A.

(Note: Read Yiddish from right to left.)

אַ מוטער האַט געזאַגט איר פיר־יעריג
טעכטערל, אַז אויב זי וועט יעדען
טאָג עסען אַ קאַשקע, וועט זי
אויסוואַקסען אַ שיינע פרוי.
באַטראַכט די קליינע איר מוטער און
פרעגט איר:
— פֿאַרוואָס־זשע האַסטו ניט געגעסען
קיין קאַשקעס וועו דו ביזט געווען
אַ קליינע? ...

A mother told her four-year-old daughter that every day she must eat a little *kashke* (porridge) so that she would grow up to be a pretty girl.

The little girl thought about it and asked her mother, "Why didn't you eat any *kashke* when you were little?"

BULGARIA

"Auntie, what are you doing with the fish?"

"I am washing them, Katie."

"Gee, I've always envied fish because they lived in the water and never had to wash!"

PAKISTAN

(Read from right to left)

پاپ (بیے سے) – جو کدچو مین لمپیی پو حجمون تمبین فوراً بتلان پرے گا ۰ احچا پاکستان کے
بابائے قوم کون کقے ؟

بیا – فورا

Father to Son: Whatever I ask, you must answer *at once*. Well, name the founder of Pakistan.

Son: At once.

BULGARIA

Mother: Stop pulling the cat's tail!

Son: I am not pulling its tail. I am just holding it, but the cat is pulling away from me!

IRAQ

Mother: Hassan, you ate all the cookies and didn't think about your brother.

Hassan: Yes, I did! I was thinking about him to come and share them with me!

ENGLAND

The Tie

My Daddy has a tie.
Can you tell me why?
To put around his neck, of course,
Just like a halter round a horse.
Lynne Wilkinson
Eleven years old

YUGOSLAVIA

»Doktore, molim vas, mora li moj brat uzimati lijek S hladnom vodom ili U hladnoj vodi?«

"Doctor, tell me please, does my brother have to take the medicine *with* the cold water or *in* the cold water?"

School Snickers

If you're reading this book, the chance is good that you've gone to school *sometime, somewhere*, for at least a little while. And anybody who's spent even a day in school knows that going to school has its up and downs. This chapter opens the door on just a few of the funny things that can happen when children and schools get together.

Watch out, Teacher—and, watch out, Mom and Dad: the joke may very well be on you! This is a book of "funnies" that *children* relish. Remember how things like these pleased *you* a hundred and fifty years ago . . . or whenever it was that you were young?

Thirty-nine different countries, in ten languages besides English, have shared their school snickers in this chapter. A cartoon, puzzles, tricks on teachers by students, joke-games, word play: there seems no end to the fun that can be found in and about school over and under the books that are propped up on the desks in schoolrooms around the world.

Is your teacher as absent-minded as the one who insisted that Maier speak for himself? Was the Small Voice speaking in Guyana? Which answer would you choose if you had the bad luck to be late to school —one from Lebanon, one from Kenya, one from the U.S.S.R. (a pretty tricky answer, by the way!), or your own invention?

The answers to the questions found here are straight-from-the-shoulder, and quite often as pricky as a goat's-head thorn—funny, and fun to remember. Laughing about somebody else's "backtalk" can be the best safety valve on earth.

Dig in, and see how your school snickers compare with those of your 'round-the-world schoolmates!

LEBANON
(Read the original from right to left.)

— أتى تلميذان إلى الصف بعد أن ابتدأ
المعلم بشرح الدرس
— فسأل الأول
لماذا تأخرت يا طوني ؟
— فقال طوني لقد أضعت ليره يا أستاذ
— فسأل الثاني
وأنت لماذا تأخرت يا حنا ؟
فأجاب حنا كنت أدعس على الليره
يا أستاذ

———

Two students came late to class,
after the teacher had begun
the lesson.
The teacher asked the first:
"Why are you late, Tom?"
"I lost my quarter, Sir."
"Why are you late, John?"
"I was stepping on the
quarter, Sir."

?????????????????

GERMANY

Teacher: Max, why did you
laugh just now?
Max: I was thinking about
something, Teacher.
Teacher: Remember once and
for all that during school
hours you are not supposed
to think.

PORTUGAL

No Exam

—Diga lá menino: como se chamam
os animais que vivem um
tempo em terra e outro ne
água?
—Chamam-se banhistas, senhor
professor.

———

Test

Tell me, boy: What is the
name of animals who live
in and outside of water?
They are called beachboys,
teacher.

GUYANA

Sunday School Teacher: I saw you stealing Mrs. Brown's mango and I think that it was very nice of you to decide to put it back in her basket afterward. Did you hear the Small Voice (conscience) telling you that it was wrong?

Boy: No, Sir. I saw a small worm.

ETHIOPIA

The teacher was giving a lesson to students in the fifth grade. One of the students was talking. The teacher said, "Aster, you are not behaving right today. Come and kneel down here."

"All right," Aster said, and she came and knelt down. Then she asked, "Teacher, what is the opposite of 'kneel down'?"

" 'Stand up,' " answered the teacher.

"Thank you," said Aster, and went back to her seat.

THAILAND

A boy comes to the office of the school principal to get his help.

Dang: My brother has been fighting and he has been hit very hard.

Principal: Where is he now?

Dang: Right on the corner of the school grounds.

Principal: And how long has this fight been going on?

Dang: Half an hour, Sir.

Principal: And you just came to tell me *now?*

Dang: Up until now, my brother was winning!

NORWAY

—Du sa jo at vi kunne male det vi ville, så vi malte Berit!

"You said we could paint anything we wanted, so we painted Berit!"

IRAN

The teacher in the classroom was saying, "Children, don't eat too many cookies and candies. Too many sweets are harmful to the body. Particularly remember that before meals you shouldn't eat sweets."

At this moment, he saw that Parri wasn't listening. He asked her, "Well, Parri, see if you can tell me when one can eat sweets."

Parri said, "When nobody is in the room and a plate of sweets is on the table."

SRI LANKA

Teacher: William, don't you ever wash yourself after your meals? Why, by looking at your mouth, I can even tell you ate eggs this morning.

William: Yes, Teacher, I had eggs for breakfast, but that was yesterday. Today I ate rice.

IRELAND

Teacher: Why are there no more cannibals?

Student: Somebody ate them . . .

CANADA

"Where was the American Declaration of Independence signed?"

"At the bottom of the page."

———————

—Où a été signée la Déclaration de l'Indépendence Américaine?

—Au bas de la page.

SIERRA LEONE

Teacher: What are the chief minerals of Sierra Leone?

Boy: Lemonade and ginger beer, Sir.

One of the favorite forms of verse fun in schools around the world is the limerick. Below are some samples as "teasers." How many others do you know? Also here are some of the countless variants of "Mary had a little lamb . . ." Is yours here?

ENGLAND

A young engine driver at Crewe
Put chewing-gum into the flue.
A boy standing by
Said, "Now I know why
"The engine says chew-chew,
    chew-chew."
             John Anderson,
             Northumberland

NIGERIA

There was a young girl called
    Lana
Who went with her father to
    Ghana.
She said to her pa,
"What I like in Accra,
It's so easy to get a banana!"
             Laoulath King
             Form IIIP, Fon

AUSTRALIA

Mary had a little lamb.
Her father shot it dead.
And now it goes to school
    with her
Between two chunks of bread!

U.S.A.

Mary had a little lamb.
His feet were black as soot.
And into Mary's bread and jam
His sooty foot he put.
             Students at Maedgen
             School, Lubbock, Texas

ENGLAND

Mary had a parrot.
It talked to her all day.
Between them both,
They said so much,
There's nothing more
    to say.
             Josie Francis, Age 12

LEBANON

A teacher asked a student to draw a fish in the sea on a piece of paper. The student drew a fish without the sea.

"Why didn't you draw the sea?"

"The paper would get wet."

U.S.S.R.

HA HA HA

Teacher: Ivan, you are late to school again!

Ivan: Yes, Comrade Teacher, but it is never too late to learn.

EGYPT

HA HA HA HA HA

The teacher asked her pupils:

"Which of you would like to go to Paradise?"

All the pupils but one raised their hands. The teacher asked the boy in question:

"Why don't you want to go to Paradise?"

"I wish I could, Teacher, but I am going to the movies tonight."

HA HA HA HA HA

IRAQ

Teacher: Why are you shivering, Abdul? It's warm in the classroom.

Abdul: It's just that zero on my test paper!

HA HA HA HO HA HA HA HA HA HA HA HO HO HO HA HA

IRAN

A pupil said to his teacher, "Yesterday you said five and five made ten, and today you tell me that seven and three make ten. Which one am I supposed to believe?"

SCOTLAND

HA HA HA HA HA

Teacher: Name one animal that lives in Lapland.

Student: A reindeer.

Teacher: Good. Next! You name another

Second Student: Another reindeer.

NEW ZEALAND

A teacher had been lecturing his pupils on the virtues of being trustworthy. "Now," he said, "we'll start the exam. Please take your seats three meters apart from one another."

SWITZERLAND

A child had been bad at school, so he had to write this on the blackboard ten times: "The teacher says, Bill has been bad."

But Bill wrote, "The teacher, says Bill, has been bad." "The teacher, says Bill, has been bad." "The teacher, . . ."

MALAYSIA

Teacher: What is only skin-deep?
Student: Dirt, Sir.

JAMAICA

Teacher: Henry, can you tell us what the shape of our earth is?

Henry: Yes, Teacher. It's square.

Teacher: Oh, no. Henry. It's *round*. See. Here is a globe . . .

Henry: Then why do people always say tourists travel to the four *corners* of the world?

ITALY

The teacher questions Pierino.
"What is a biography?"
"The life story of a man."
"And what is topography?"
"The life story of a mouse."

(Note: Topo means "mouse" in Italian)

BRAZIL

O inventor da locomotiva foi George Stephenson. A primeira locomotiva era pequena e fraca e em quase nada se parecia com as atuais. Em 1830, o primeiro trem à vapor fez o percurso de Liverpool à Manchester. Tubinho, você sabe onde foi que rodou o primeiro trem à vapor?

  Tubinho: Sei...
  Então diga!
  Tubinho: Nos trilhos!

_____

The inventor of the locomotive was George Stephenson. The first locomotive was small and narrow and hardly looked like the ones of today. In 1830, the first steam engine went from Liverpool to Manchester. Tubinho, do you know where the first steam engine ran?

  Tubinho: Yes...
Then tell me!
  Tubinho: On the tracks!

(Tubinho is a favorite Brazilian character in a cartoon-strip series "Tubinho.")

THAILAND

ไม่เคยคิด

นักเรียน: - คุณครู, ผมไม่คิดว่าครูจะให้วิบ่าบของผมอู่นย์

ครู: - ฉันเองก็ไม่เคยคิดเป่นนั้น แต่ไม่ยีใครต่ำกว่านี้.

วอลาดา
28 จุฬาซ่อย 16 พระยาไทย
กรุงเทพุ 5

_____

I Never Thought

Student: Teacher, I never thought you would give me a zero in this subject.

Teacher: I never thought so, either, but there is no lower mark.

Vorada, 28 Chula Soi, 16 Phya Thai, Bangkok 5

CANADA

Teacher: John, how do you spell "Saskatchewan"?

John: Do you want the river or the province?

SYRIA

Teacher: Ali, when do you like school the best?

Ali: When it's closed, Sir.

EGYPT

Ahmed: Bad news! Imagine! I failed seven subjects this semester.

Ali: Thank God! You *could* have failed *eight* subjects.

Ahmed: There were only seven.

IRELAND

Pupil: Teacher did you know that a cat has three tails?

Teacher: That can't be so. No cat has even *two* tails.

Pupil: But, Teacher, if *no* cat has *two* tails and *one* cat has *one* tail, and if *one* cat plus *no* cat equals *one* cat, and *one* tail plus *two* tails equals *three* tails, then one cat has three tails!

NEW ZEALAND

Teacher: John, why aren't you listening?

John: But, teacher, I *am* listening!

Teacher: If you were listening, tell me what I said.

John: You said, "John, why aren't you listening?"

CANADA

Teacher: When is the best time to pick the fruit from the trees?

Stuart: When the watchman is not there!

KENYA

"Ūcereirūo nīkī ūmūthī?" mūrutani akīūria mūrutwo.

Mūrutwo nake akīmūcokeria, "Githī ndūūī mbura yurīte ūtukū mūgima; na njīra ītendenderete nginya atī ngūkinyūkagia ikinya rīmwe mbere, ngatenderūka merī thutha."

Mūrutani afīīra mūrutwo, "Rūciū wona kūrī gūtenderū, ūkambīrīria gūthiī werekeire na mwena ūcio ūngī, na ndūgacererūo nī cukuru."

———————

"Why were you late for class?" the teacher asked the pupil.

The boy answered, "You know it has rained all night; the road is so wet and slippery that for every step I made forward, I slipped backward two steps."

"If it is as wet tomorrow," the teacher advised the pupil, "start walking in the opposite direction and you will get to school on time."

AUSTRIA

Der kleine Peter besuchte seine Lehrerin, die krank zu Hause war. Als er wieder aus dem Haus kam, warteten Klassenkameraden auf ihn. Er schüttelte den Kopf: keine Hoffnung, keine Hoffnung, sie kommt morgen wieder zur Schule.

———————

Little Peter visited his teacher, who was ill at home. As he came back out of the house, his classmates were waiting for him. He shook his head: "No hope, no hope; she will be coming back to school tomorrow."

BULGARIA

— Тошко, защо си поставил памук в ухото си? Боли ли те?
— Не, но нали ни казахте, каквото влезе в едното ухо, да не излиза от другото.

———————

Teacher: Tony, why do you have cotton in your ear? Does it hurt?
Tony: No, Teacher, but you always tell me what goes in one ear comes out from the other!

A popular form of school humor worldwide is found in problems and puzzles set by one child for another. Some of these have "trick" answers, while others require careful listening or sound logic. How many of your own puzzles can you add to the ones on this page and on pages 31 and 32?

BOTSWANA

A man has three things: a rat, some seeds, and a cat. He wants to take them across the river, but he is not able, because of good sense, to take all of them at the same time. What should he do? If he takes the cat, the rat will remain to eat the seeds; if he takes the seeds and leaves the cat and the rat, the cat will eat the rat.

He can take the seeds and the rat, cross the river with them, leave the seeds and go back with the rat, leave the rat and take the cat across, and go back to get the rat.

BURMA

There was a mango tree in U Min's yard. One day, suspecting the children in the neighborhood would try to climb his tree for those delicious ripe fruits, he left his pet monkey out in the tree to guard it. This kept the children away from the tree—at least, *most* of the children. However, it did not bother Maung Tu, who thought of a brilliant idea to get U Min's mangoes. What did he do?

He threw stones at the monkey, who became very angry and threw mangoes back at Maung Tu.

INDIA

How is it possible for Raghu to stand behind Prabhu and for Prabhu to stand behind Raghu at the same time?

They can stand back to back.

NIGERIA

A man has 19 cows which he wants to share out among his three sons so that the first son gets 1/2 of the cows, the second 1/4 of the cows, and the third 1/5 of the cows. How does he carry out this plan without killing or giving away any of the cows?

He must borrow a cow, making the cows he has 20. Then he gives 1/2 of 20 to his first son. That is 10. Then he gives the third and the second 1/5 and 1/4 of 20 which will be 4 and 5. Ten plus 4 plus 5 equals 19. He therefore gives back the borrowed cow.

Irene Onyemenam
Form IVP

INDIA

How may times can you subtract the numeral "one" from the numeral "twenty-nine"?

Only once. After the first time you are subtracting from twenty-eight, then twenty-seven, and so on.

??????? ??? ??????? ??? ??? ???

LESOTHO

Monna o na le liphoofolo tse tharo, Lenqau, Tau le Poli. O na le sekepe se le seng feela, se ka nkang batho ba ba beli feela, joale o batla ho tšelisa liphoofolo tsena tsa hae noka empa e tletse, joale o tšoanela ho sebelisa sekepe, empa Lenqau le ja Poli, me Tau e ja Lenqau, o tla litšelisa joang?

O tla tšelisa Lenqau pele, a khutle a nke Tau a e tšelise, ebe o khutla le Lenqau, a fihle a nke Poli a e tšelise, e be o qetella ka ho tšelisa Lenqau.

———

A man has three animals, a leopard, a lion, and a goat. He wants to take them across a river that is in flood, but since he has only one boat, with the capacity of two persons at a time, and since the leopard feeds on goats and the lion feeds on leopards and he cannot leave them safely alone together, how can he manage to carry them across the river?

He can take the leopard across first, return to take the lion across, unload the lion and take back the leopard, unload the leopard and take the goat across, and finally come back to get the leopard.

MARTINIQUE

"My children," the teacher says, "I've just taught you the conjugation with all the tenses: the present, the past, the future. Do you understand? Let's see. Albert?"

Albert thought that by hiding behind a tall boy he wouldn't have to answer.

"Albert, if I say, 'I wash, you wash, he washes, we wash, you wash, they wash,' what is it?"

"Well, Miss, it's Sunday."

AUSTRALIA

Teacher: Where were you born?
Pupil: Sydney.
Teacher: What part?
Pupil: All of me.

UGANDA

Teacher: Mutesa, what expression do students who don't study use most of all?
Mutesa: I don't know.
Teacher: Right!

U.S.S.R.

Teacher: Aleksei, you have written a long composition, but I can't find a single comma or period in it.
Aleksei: You didn't like the way I used periods and commas the other times, so I thought you'd want to put in all the punctuation.

BELGIUM

In arithmetic class:

"Your father buys ten litres of wine at 75 francs (about $2.50) per litre. How much will it take him?"

"Oh . . . it'll take him about two days."

BULGARIA

Teacher: All things expand from the heat and contract from the cold. Who can give me an example?

Student: The days, Teacher. In winter they are short because of the cold, and in summer they are longer because of the heat!

INDIA

Ashok: What did I get for my English test?

Teacher: Well, I'll give you the good news first. You spelled your name correctly.

GERMANY

Teacher: When was Rome built?

Max: In one night.

Teacher: What makes you think that?

Max: I've heard Rome wasn't built in a day.

AUSTRIA

The absent-minded professor shouts: "Maier, come to the blackboard!"

Another student says, "Maier is absent, Mr. Professor."

"Silence! Let Maier speak for himself."

IRAN

In a grade school, during the first-grade students' mathematics exam, a teacher asked one of the students to write the number "eleven."

The student wrote the number "one" and didn't show any movement toward making the second "one."

"Why are you waiting?" the teacher asked.

"I'm just wondering where to put the second 'one'—on the left or on the right!"

SINGAPORE

Asked to write a rhyme beginning with the line, "Sing a song of sixpence," three budding poets came out with the following:

From a boy complaining about his pocket money (allowance):

> Sing a song of sixpence,
> A pocket full of holes;
> What with all the inflation,
> That's where my money goes!

From a history student:

> Sing a song of sixpence,
> History lessons are a bore;
> With whatever little that I cram in,
> I seem to forget more and more.

From a problem kid in class:

> Sing a song of sixpence,
> An example, my case is made out to be;
> Four and twenty hundred lines I've to write—
> Oh, my hands are killing me.

THAILAND

In class, the teacher showed the pictures of various birds. Then he asked one of the students a question.

> Teacher: What kind of bird do you like best?
> Piak: Fried chicken, Sir.

U.S.A.

"Where is your pencil, George?"

"I ain't got one."

"Say, 'I haven't a pencil.'"

"Gee, where *are* all the pencils?"

FRANCE

"Sir," the teacher says to the father of one of his pupils, "I've asked you to come because I've discovered somewhat of a problem with your son: I have proof that he cheats in his tests."

"That is impossible," the father answers. "My son Pierre does not copy anyone else's work. Sir, you are mistaken, if you will pardon my saying so."

"May I show you proof so that we can both be sure? For example, here is a history test; the answers are copied from the paper of his friend Henri. See the first answers on both papers. The question: Who followed Napoleon? Henri's answer: Louis XVIII; Pierre's answer: Louis XVIII."

"Aha!" exclaimed the father. "But it *was* Louis XVIII."

"True," admitted the teacher. "But see the second answers. The question: Where did Napoleon have his biggest victory? Henri's answer: London; Pierre's answer: London."

"Yes, I see them both . . . but it's purely coincidence. That's not sufficient proof to accuse my son of copying!"

"Wait, Sir, until you see the third answers. The question: Where did Napoleon die? Henri's answer: I don't know; Pierre's answer: me either."

Goons and Goofs

What are "goons"? In this chapter, they are funny-foolish people (or other animals). And what are "goofs"? Here, they are funny-foolish mistakes.

We have all been goons at one time or another, so it's fun to find somebody who's a bigger goon than we are. As for goofs, you'd run out of fingers and toes before you finished counting your own goofs. That's why you laugh when you read about bigger goofs than yours. Goons and goofs are funny because they're outside ourselves and we feel lucky enough to laugh.

The funniest thing about goons and goofs, though, is their worldwide distribution. The languages are different; the faces are different; the places are different; but we're clearly all in the "goons and goofs" business together.

Goons and goofs from thirty-eight countries, in ten languages besides English, are tucked into this chapter. Can you find a goon like you in Guyana or in Turkey, in Australia or in Korea? Did someone make a goof like yours—or worse!—in Hong Kong or in Ghana (that one was almost hopeless...), or in Latvia or Chile?

The chapter begins with a joke that ties "School Snickers" and "Goons and Goofs" together: the well-known stunt of "calling in, sick." (The samples from Iran and from Peru are only two of dozens that have turned up in my quest for children's jokes; you probably have your own version, not too different from these.) The Indonesian matches goof is a real "funny," and so is the English "frightfully interesting chemical experiment." It's hard to pick a favorite.

Here you will find the "dummers" who make you feel both taller and smarter: Goha jokes in Egypt are as catching as the flu, and as widespread as the van der Merwe "funnies" are in South Africa, the Rudi-and-Bobi nonsense in Yugoslavia, the Jaimito jokes in Argentina and in Puerto Rico, and the Molboer jokes in Denmark.

Whatever you're doing—maybe eating a ladybug instead of a currant—have fun!

The temptation to stay away from school on a school day is felt by children—and by teachers!—around the world. Jokes reflecting this universal feeling may be found in many countries, but the funniest ones usually involve goofs. The two given here, from Iran and Peru, are samples.

PERU

Suena el teléfono en la oficina del Director del colegio.
 —Aló, ¿puedo hablar con el Director?
 —Con él habla.
 —Llamo para avisar que mi hijo Juanito Pérez no puede ir al colegio hoy pues está muy resfriado.
 —¿Quien habla, por favor?
 —Mi papá.

The telephone rings in the office of the Principal at the high school.
 "Hello, may I speak to the Principal?"
 "This is the Principal speaking."
 "I am calling to advise you that my son Johnny Smith cannot go to school today because he has a cold."
 "Who is speaking, please?"
 "My father."

(Note: In Peru the name "Juanito Pérez" is as commonly used as is "Johnny Smith" in the United States.)

IRAN

من پدرم هستم

درینگ ! درینگ ! تلفن دبستان زنگ هی زند • مدیر گوشی را بر می دارد •

مدیر : هَلو !

— : هَلو ، آقای مدیر سلام •

مدیر : سلام ، بفرمایید ، کاری داشتید ؟

— : بله ، می خواستم بگویم رضا امروز سرما خورده است ، و نمی تواند به

مدرسه بیاید •

مدیر : بِبخشید ، شماکی هستید ؟

— : من •• من ، آقا ••• پدرم هستم •

I Am My Father

Dring! Dring! The telephone at the elementary school rings, and the principal picks up the receiver.

Principal: Hello!

"Hello, Mr. Principal. Peace. Salaam."

Principal: Salaam. May I help you?

"Yes, I wanted to tell you that today Reza has caught a cold and he can't come to school."

Principal: Pardon me. Who are you?

"Me . . . Sir . . . I'm my father."

AUSTRALIA

Patient: Doc, I'm suffering
    from amnesia.
Doctor: How long have you
    had it?
Patient: Had what?

CZECHOSLOVAKIA

Mr. Kužel's car ran over
Vonáseks' cat, so he went over
to apologize.

"I would like to make up
somehow for that cat, Mrs.
Vonásek."

"O.K. Come over tonight and
catch mice!"

INDONESIA

Mother sent her son Ali to the
store across the street to buy a
good box of matches.

When Ali came back, Mother
asked him: Did you buy a
good box of matches?
Ali: Yes, Mother. I have tried
them all.

PUERTO RICO

Jaimito (talking to an angry
    man whose window he had
    just broken): Pardon me,
    Sir, but have you seen my
    soccer ball?

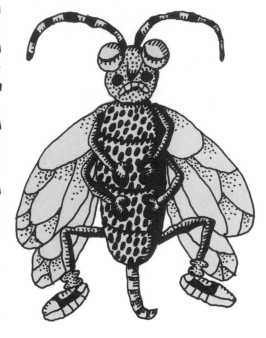

BOTSWANA

Monna wa Sematla

Gatwe erile ka tsatsi le lengwe
sesupanako. Sa monna sa senyega
ga a se bula a fitlhela ntsi ee suleng
e le moteng a ba are, "Oo!
Makhenekhe o sule; ke selo
sesupanako same se sa tsamaye."

The Foolish Fellow

One day a foolish fellow's watch
(literally, "something which
shows time") stopped working.
He opened it and found a dead
fly inside and then he said, "Oh!
The operator is dead; that's why
my watch is not working."

EGYPT

ا ابو النواس ناد على جحا يا جحا حد سرق

صندوق مجوهراتك .

جحا ضحك وقال معلش يا أبو النواس

أنا معاي المفتاح .

Abu el Nawas called after his friend Goha, "Hey, Goha! Someone has stolen your treasure box."

Goha smiled. "Don't worry, Abu. I have the key."

ZAMBIA

Nkumbula: Why did Fwanya bring a pistol to the basketball game?

Lewanika: Because the coach told him that tonight he'd finally get a chance to shoot the ball!

YUGOSLAVIA

"Careful, there!" "Careful, there, I say!" "I told you to move away!"

LAOS

Once a beggar, who was too lazy to work, but lived daily on the kindnesses of others, received from a neighbor a large jar of rice. Putting the jar on the table, he then sat down in front of it and thought hard about what he would do with this unexpected treasure. At last, he had a fine idea:

"I'll wait till a famine comes," said he to himself, "and then I'll sell this rice for much money. With the money, I'll buy me a pair of cows, and when they have a calf, I'll sell it for a pair of buffaloes. When the buffaloes have a calf, I'll sell them, find me a wife, and have a grand wedding. When we have a child large enough to sit up by himself, I'll take care of him while my wife works the fields. If she says, 'Indeed, I'll *not* work in the fields,' I'll kick her *hard*, like this!"

He kicked with all his might, and over went the table and jar. It broke, of course, and the rice spilled through the cracks in the floor. Along came the neighbors' pigs to eat it. Now, what can he do with that broken jar?

TURKEY

İkl deli oturuyorlardı. Biri öbürüne, "Söyle bakalım avcumda ne var?" dedi.
İkinci deli, "Fil," diye cevap verdi.
Arkadası, "Bu sayılmaz çünkü gördün," diye bağırdı.

————————

Two fools were sitting. One of them asked the other, "Tell me what you think I have in my hand?"

The other fool answered, "An elephant."

His friend shouted, "That one doesn't count, because you saw it."

THAILAND

Uncle Um went to buy a bottle of lotion from the drugstore for treating a rash. On the way home, he remembered that he had forgotten to ask one very important question. He hurried back to ask the druggist:

"This medicine that I bought to cure my rash . . . do I apply it *before* or *after* meals?"

Tonchai Pinyakul

CZECHOSLOVAKIA

Mother is very impatient. Honza (Johnny) should have been home from school long ago. Finally he arrives and his mother asks, "Where were you all this time? Didn't I tell you to come straight home from school?"

"But Mommy," he explains, "we couldn't help it; we were doing a good deed."

"Well, then, I'll forgive you this time. What was your good deed?"

"We helped an old lady across the street."

"And that took you all this time?"

"Well, yes. You see, she really didn't want to cross the street at all."

IRAN

During which season of the year should a room with 12 windows be used?

During winter, of course. It's very clear. If a room has one window, closing that one window keeps the room warm. If you close 12 windows, the room would stay 12 times as warm. That way, it would be exactly right for winter.

KUWAIT

"Yesterday I went to the dentist to see about my aching tooth."

"Is it still hurting?"

"Just a minute, while I call the dentist to find out. He kept it."

U.S.A.

Diner: What kind of pie is this?

Waitress: What does it taste like, Sir?

Diner: It tastes like glue.

Waitress: Well, then, it's peach; the apple pie tastes like putty.

ECUADOR

Iban dos niños viajando en tren. Uno de los dos estaba sentado junto a la ventana y veía que los árboles se movían muy rápido. Entonces le dice al amigo: "Al regreso venimos en árbol."

Two children were traveling by train. One of them was sitting by the window and saw that the trees were moving very fast. He turned to his friend and said, "Going back, we'll take a tree instead of the train."

CHILE

A woman had three dogs, one called "Earthquake," another called "Tidal Wave," and the other called "Lie."

One day the dogs ran away from the woman. The woman began to call: "Earthqua-a-ake!" All the people got very scared and began running.

Then she cried out, "Tidal Wa-a-ave!" All the people started climbing up the trees from fright.

Then she called out, "Li-i-ie!" And then the people went and hit the woman.

Sergio Ruis Tagle,
Age 8

DENMARK

Erik: Today I received an anonymous letter.
Jens: So? Who was it from?

POLAND

Two girls were watching the sparrows eating food at a bird feeder. The younger girl asked:

"I wonder what the sparrows eat when they can't find food in the bird feeder?"

"Then they eat what they can find," replied the older one.

"What happens when they don't find anything?"

"Then they eat something else."

INDIA

षेर्ष पिल्की रेडीग्रो भुव २ट्टी थी। रेडीग्रोमें एक एउ एउवरयइज्ञमेल्ण श्स प्रकार का आया:।केसी भी तरट्ट के टुाटवे पर षरवॉँष्ठ ष्ठभारये। उसी सय पिल्को की माँ २सोडे से कमरे मे आई,यट हुए कि "ड्ाय!आडा तो सब्दुगी द्ुाठ यई है"! बेबी पिल्की षे आराम र-ोअपषी मर्ग्यी कोयट यालह दी । "म२ग्रीउसमे मि यिथापा करवकी कीई षह। है । सबट्टिपर बरवॉँउ फ्या ये,सब कुध्रु ठीक उायेग्ा ।

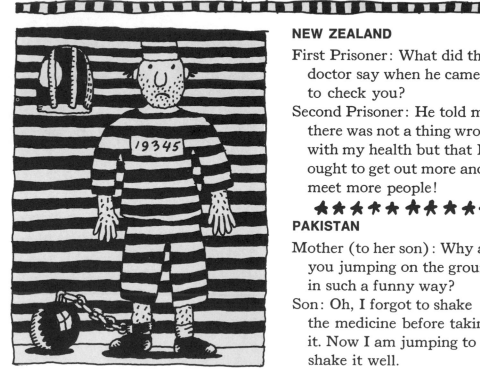

Baby Pinki was listening to the radio. One advertisement went like this: "For any type of burns, apply Burnol." At that moment, Pinki's mother came in from the kitchen, saying, "Oh! Today the vegetable is burned!" Pinki coolly told her mother, "Mother, do not worry. Apply Burnol to it, and then everything will be all right."

NEW ZEALAND

First Prisoner: What did the doctor say when he came to check you?

Second Prisoner: He told me there was not a thing wrong with my health but that I ought to get out more and meet more people!

PAKISTAN

Mother (to her son): Why are you jumping on the ground in such a funny way?

Son: Oh, I forgot to shake the medicine before taking it. Now I am jumping to shake it well.

KOREA

A simple-minded fellow went to the United States to visit relatives. When he got back home, his neighbors all gathered at his house to hear about his trip.

"Well, when I landed in New York City, I went right away to see the Empire State Building. Funny thing, though . . . when I came out of the building, a city fellow sitting on a bench across the way got up and said, 'How many floors did you see?' "

'Fifty,' I answered.

" 'Aha!' he said. 'That will cost you fifty dollars. You know, everyone who visits this building has to pay for every floor he sees.' So I paid him."

" You mean you paid 25,000 *won* (the Korean equivalent of fifty dollars) just to see that building?" His neighbors laughed. "He was cheating you . . . "

"Oh, but I had the last laugh," the traveler interrupted. "I *really* saw the whole building!"

(Note: An old trick played by New York city slickers—and by tricksters elsewhere in the world, as well—on visitors is to sell them the Brooklyn Bridge or the Empire State Building or the Bronx Zoo or some other famous site.)

TURKEY

A small child was giving a bath to a tiny kitten in the garden. An old lady passing by said, "Sonny, you shouldn't bathe a kitty in cold water. He'll get sick and die."

But the boy went on with his job, barely listening to her.

Two hours later, the lady was returning when she saw the boy sitting on the ground and crying, with the dead kitten lying beside him.

"Didn't I tell you, sonny, that the kitty would die if you washed him in the cold water?"

"But Auntie, he didn't die because I washed him; he died when I was wringing him dry."

(Note: "Auntie" is used here as a term of respect, as "Uncle" is used in China.)

SOUTH AFRICA

The telephone was ringing, and van der Merwe answered it.

"Is this Mr. Smith?" a lady asked.

"No," answered van der Merwe.

"Oh, sorry. Wrong number."

"Ah, it's O.K.," said van der Merwe. "The phone was ringing anyway."

RRRINGG

URUGUAY

(In the movies.)

A fat man got up from his seat and left during the intermission. When he returned, in the dark, since the movie had already started, he politely asked the man right next to his seat:

"Tell me, Sir, when I left, did I step on you?"

"Yes," answered the other coldly, expecting an apology.

"Oh, good!" said the fat man with a sigh. "Then this is my row."

BOTSWANA

One time in conversation a foolish man heard someone else say, "My watch runs very well."

"Watch?" he thought. "I don't have a watch." And the next time he went to Mafikeng, he bought a watch.

After he got out of the shop, he put the watch on the ground and said, "Now, run home. I'll meet you there shortly."

AUSTRALIA

First Chum: Did you hear about the poor bloke who made himself a new boomerang?

Second Chum: No. What happened to him?

First Chum: He went crazy trying to throw the old one away!

ITALY

Pierino: Daddy, do you like
    baked apples?
Daddy: Yes. Why?
Pierino: The orchard is burning.

———————

Pierino: Papà, ti piacciono le mele
    cotte?
Papà: Sì. Perché?
Pierino: Brucia il frutteto.

CZECHOSLOVAKIA

Peter suddenly became very
quiet and then piped up,
"Daddy, do currants have little
legs?"

    "Where would currants get
legs? What gave you that idea?"

    "No? Then I must have eaten
a ladybug."

LEBANON

A foolish man was walking on a
street in the city when the street
suddenly curved to the left. He
didn't notice but kept walking
straight ahead until he walked
right into a tall building.

    "Why, this building shouldn't
be here," he said. "I'll move it."

    Taking off his jacket and
laying it on the ground, he
started pushing. While he was
pushing, a thief took his jacket.
When the man looked back, he
didn't see his jacket.

    "My goodness," he said. "I
pushed it much too far. I should
move it back a bit." And again
he started pushing . . .

AUSTRALIA

A goofy fellow went into a
shooting gallery at a fun fair,
and shot down six ducks. The
man behind the stall gave him a
little live turtle, and the goof
went away. After a while, the
goof came back, and shot down
six ducks again. This time, the
proprietor gave him a kewpie
doll for a prize.

    "Don't give me that," said
the goof. "I want one of those
beaut crunchy pies you gave me
last time!"

ARGENTINA

Pedro: Did you hear? Jaimito has stopped making ice to sell.

Juan: Yes. He said the old lady who knew the recipe died.

VIETNAM

A simple-minded fellow went to a soccer game with a friend. After a while, he had an idea of the game:

"Those soccer players are very poor, aren't they?"

"What makes you think so?"

"They must not have enough money to buy a ball for each of them so they keep fighting to get the one they have!"

FINLAND

The judge asked the man, "Can you read and write?"

"I can write, but I can't read, Sir."

"Then write your name there, please."

The man wrote something on the paper.

"What did you write?" asked the astounded judge.

"I don't know," replied the man. "I told you I don't know how to read."

YUGOSLAVIA

Bobi had one weird habit: Every evening before going to bed, he would spit through the window and then jump into his bed.

One morning, his friend Rudi found him lying on the grass under the window of his bedroom. "What are you doing here? I thought you'd still be in bed."

Bobi rubbed his eyes. "Ha, ha!" laughed Bobi. "You know my weird habit. Well, last night I must have spat into my bed and then jumped out the window!"

ZAÏRE

Dumba, the New-style Peanut Planter

On another day, Dumba's older sister set out for her garden to plant peanuts.

"Wait right here, Sister," Dumba said proudly. "*I'll* plant the peanuts this time. You're so old-fashioned about planting peanuts. You'll see the difference when you taste *my* crop."

"How are you going to plant our peanuts, my clever brother?" she asked. "There's only one right way to plant them . . ." But Dumba had already gone off, with the peanut basket hung snugly on his back. That Dumba . . .

The sun was setting when Dumba returned, walking tall and smiling to himself. The basket was empty.

"Well, how did you ?"

"Shhh! No questions, please. You'll see when the peanuts are harvested," said Dumba. And not another word would he say.

As the time for harvest neared, all the other peanut fields were green. As for Dumba's field, the ground was as bare as his hand. Peanuts? Not a leaf was showing.

Finally, his sister *had* to know. "Dumba, what *is* this new style of planting?"

"Well, Sister, it's very simple: to save the trouble of roasting our peanuts afterwards, I roasted them before I planted them. Think how good they will taste!"

"*You* try them, you clever new-style planter," said his sister, laughing in spite of the lost peanuts. And while Dumba dug up the small handful of withered peanuts that were still in the ground where he had put them, his sister hurried to the market to trade for peanuts from those who had planted the old-fashioned way.

(The tale, originally told in Lonkundo, begins the way folktales among the Nkundo usually
   begin: "On another day, . . .")

DENMARK

One summer when the corn was well grown, a stork decided to make his home in the Molbo field. He walked back and forth catching frogs, but the Molboers thought he was trampling down a great deal of corn, so they wanted to be rid of him. They took counsel among themselves and decided to ask the village herder to chase the stork out.

But when he was to go after the stork, they became aware that his feet were much larger and wider than those of the stork and thus he would destroy more corn than the stork would. So they took counsel again. Among them was one wise old man who thought they should carry the herder through the corn. They all decided this was good advice, so they went out and eight men carried the herder through the corn to drive the stork out. Thus the herder did not trample down any corn.

AFGHANISTAN

Three fools were sitting next to a tree close to the sea, and they were talking. After a long time of thinking, one of them said, "If the sea should catch fire, where would the fish go?"

The second one said, "That's easy. They'd climb this tree."

The third one said, "How stupid can you be? Fish are not like cows and oxen, who climb trees!"

IRAN

Iraj was ready to write a letter to his friend, who was on a trip. His mother asked, "What are you doing?"

"I am writing a letter to Hasan."

"Do you know his address?"

"No. He's on vacation. At the end of the letter I will ask him to send me his address."

DENMARK

How can one know which mushrooms are poisonous?

One finds it out the next day!

—Hvordan kan man vide, om svampene er giftige?

—Det maerker man dagen efter!

GUYANA

Richard was not too smart, so everyone played tricks on him. One dark night, some of the boys dared him to climb up on the beam of their flashlight. Richard thought about it for a while. Then he said, "You think that I am stupid, but I am not. If I climb that beam, you will let me reach the top of it and then you will switch the light off and I will fall down."

ROMANIA

A little boy standing in front of the wolf's cage is throwing rocks at him. An angry zoo guard runs up to him and asks, "What are you doing? What did that poor wolf do to you?"

"Comrade, he didn't do anything to *me*. But don't you remember? He ate up Little Red Riding Hood!"

INDIA

Ahmed: Doctor, a year ago when I had that infection in my foot, you told me not to get it wet.

Doctor: That's true, Ahmed. What's your problem now?

Ahmed: I wanted to know if it's all right now for me to wash my foot.

HONG KONG

One day two strong but simple-minded fellows were hired to move a big empty box to a store two blocks away. It wasn't too heavy for two men to carry but it was very awkward to lift. The first fellow rubbed his hands on his trousers, bent down, grabbed hold of the box, and lifted. He couldn't move the box at all. "Come on!" he called to his partner. "Lift your side when I lift mine!"

Again, he rubbed his hands on his trousers, bent down, grabbed hold of the box, and strained to lift it. He *still* couldn't move it. "Say!" he called. "Lift harder!"

When his third effort failed, he went around on the other side of the box to show his partner how to grab the box. His partner wasn't there . . . or anywhere in sight. "Hello!" he called. "Where are you?"

"I'm inside the box," his friend answered. "I figured that if you were going to lift from the outside, I'd lift from the inside!"

SIERRA LEONE

John: What is this board for?
Mary: It is a signboard.
John: Oh! I haven't got a pen with me to sign my name.

NIGERIA

Doctor: Did you follow my directions to drink water thirty minutes before going to bed?
Patient: I tried, Doctor, but I was completely full after only five minutes!

GHANA

A houseboy from another tribe living in the household with the pregnant wife of his master had to take the wife to the maternity home when she was ready to give birth. Not long after they had arrived there, the mistress gave birth to a baby boy. The houseboy was asked to tell the family members the good news. But see what happened:

Houseboy: Mi maami we wu! (My mother is dead!)

Family: We wu? (Is she dead?)

Houseboy: Aaai, we wu! (Yes, she is dead!)

Family: Breben? Ehi fa? (When? Where?)

Houseboy: See seaa. (Just a moment ago.)

(During all this time, the houseboy was happy and excited, but the family was greatly disturbed.)

Family. Wo se *wa* wu anaase *we* wu? (Did you say *she has given birth* or *she is dead?*)

Houseboy (finally realizing the mistake in his words): *We* wu akwadaa. (I said *she is dead*, but I meant *she has given birth to a child*.)

The family then became greatly excited, all talking at once, and rushed to the maternity home to see the new baby.

(Note the big difference in meaning between *we wu* and *wa wu!*)

Animal Antics

Animals, judging from children's jokes, are just people with made-to-order clothes: fur, fins, or feathers. And *is* the human animal the only one with the gift of laughter? Grin with that skinny stray dog as he eludes the dogcatcher; hear the rabbit chuckle between crunches on that carrot he "earned" from the snowman; cool off with the dog in the refrigerator as he has the last laugh on his master; chortle with Spider as he sells that big "dog," and with his Netherlands Antilles cousin Compa Nanzi as he outwits the king.

Whether animals are laughing themselves or whether they're stirring laughter in us, they appear in jokes and riddles and verses on all six continents, and spill over into every other chapter of this book. "Animal Antics" provides a "zoo" only for the jokes most clearly animal-centered.

Twenty-six countries, in four languages besides English, have shared their dogs and sardines and cats and bears and centipedes with us here. Would you send a centipede to fetch anything for a party, or put him on a soccer team? Could your runaway dog dodge the dogcatcher? What does a bear do when he can't sleep during the winter? Have you ever taken a crocodile to the movies? Or even a fish? How does the rooster know when it's time to crow? And when you're "counting sheep" at bedtime, do they ever talk back to you, as one did to Mafalda? (Mafalda, by the way, is one of the most popular cartoon characters in all of Central and South America. You'll find her again in "Fun with Friends.")

The poems from the Philippines and from Sierra Leone and the centipede comic strip from Chile are the only items in this chapter actually created and published by children themselves. Other original pieces, captured in Chile, England, Iran, Nigeria, Singapore, and the United States, appear elsewhere in the book. Do *you* have any good "funnies" to send along?

LATVIAN

A goat was drinking at a river. When he had had enough, he thumped his foot on the ground and shouted, "Not even the wolf himself can make me worry!"

The wolf, lying in the bushes, heard the words of the goat and asked, "How's that, again, Andrew? What was it you were saying?"

"Oh, honorable master of the woods," replied the goat, "when I have drunk, I use a drunkard's language!"

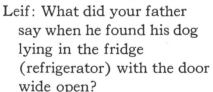

FRANCE

A young sardine was swimming along with his parents. Suddenly he was shocked to see a submarine submerge.

"You don't need to be afraid of that," said his father. "It's just a box of preserved men!"

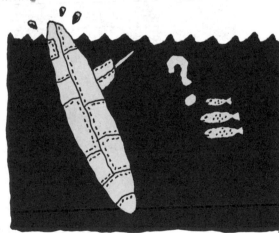

NORWAY

Leif: What did your father say when he found his dog lying in the fridge (refrigerator) with the door wide open?
Magnus: Was he mad! He said, "Why can't you lie down in the shade to cool off, like other dogs do?"

CZECHOSLOVAKIA

John: Barbie, do you know what this tiger would say if he could talk?
Barbie: Of course I know. He would tell you that he is not a tiger, but a lion!

IRAN

A lion was passing through a jungle. Of each animal that he passed, he asked, "Who is the strongest animal in the jungle?"

The animals, shivering and afraid, would say, "Your Majesty, indeed, *you*." And then the lion would nod his head and pass on.

Finally he came to an elephant. The lion asked the elephant, "Who is the strongest animal in the jungle?"

The elephant put his trunk around the lion's waist, picked him up from the ground, twirled him around, and threw him down hard onto the ground.

The lion got up, shook himself a little, and said, "Brother, I asked you a question. If you don't know the answer, say so!"

U.S.S.R.

Ivan: Where did that rabbit find a fresh carrot in the middle of winter?

Leonid: He must be some smart rabbit! He found my snowman with a carrot for a nose. Somehow, he dug up a magnifying glass, held it between the sunlight and my snowman, and melted the snowman down till he could get at the carrot.

ITALY

Pio: I hear that when Mario went camping last week, he sat up all night *outside* his tent. How come?

Carlo: Well, there was a bear sleeping in his tent, and the signboard read, "It is forbidden to disturb the animals in the park."

BRAZIL

"Why doesn't Juan walk his dog Fluffy the way we walk *our* dogs?"

"He'd like to, but Fluffy's so hairy he can't tell which end to put the collar on!"

CANADA

Why is the letter *K* like a pig's tail?

Because it is the end of por*k*.

U.S.A.

Algie saw a bear.
The bear saw Algie.
The bear was bulgy.
The bulge was Algie.

U.S.A.

Rick: How come that skinny little stray dog never gets picked up by the fellows at the animal shelter?

Dick: Every time the dog-pound truck comes by, he stands up on his hind legs behind a street signpost, and the driver never even sees him!

PAKISTAN

Calf to Mother Buffalo: Mummy! Today I want you to jump many times.

Mother Buffalo: But why, my child?

Calf: Because I want to have a milk shake today.

BANGLADESH

One day a man went to a small teashop and ordered a cup of tea. When the tea was served, he saw a fly swimming in it. Annoyed, he called the waiter and asked, "Why does this tea have a fly in it?"

The waiter said, "For a tea which costs only two *annas,* what do you expect to fall into it—an elephant?"

U.S.S.R.

Fox: My, but you're fat. You must be going to hibernate now. But why are you carrying that TV set?

Bear: Well, sometimes during the winter I have such terrible insomnia . . .

ARGENTINA

Mother: Mafalda, why did you cry out "Six!" last night after you went to bed?

Mafalda: I was counting sheep to get to sleep, and I fell asleep just after counting the "twenty" of "twenty-six." The silly twenty-sixth sheep was standing on the fence waiting to jump over, and he bleated; "*¡Be-eee!*" until I yelled "Six." Then he jumped off and I went back to sleep.

LIBERIA

The Cat

Out goes the cat.
Out goes the rat.
Out goes the lady
With a big fat bat,
To kill the rat.
But she missed the rat
And killed the cat.
Up blows her hat
And lands on the mat.
And that was the end
Of the poor old cat.

Edwin Morgan, Age 12
Grade 5

CHILE

Fiesta.

1. En una gran fiesta de animales...

2. empezó a acabarse el vino. Entonces el caballo mando al ciempiés a buscarlo...

3. Pero pasó algún rato y los amigos se fueron yendo...

4. Después de horas llegó el ciempiés con el vino y le dijo el caballo: ¿Por qué te demoraste tanto?

5. A lo que el ciempiés contesto: —¡Bah! ¿Uno no puede pasar a lastrarse los zapatos, acaso?

Feast

1. In a great animal feast...
2. the wine began to run low. Then the horse sent the centipede to buy more wine.
3. But time passed and the invited friends went away.
4. After several hours the centipede arrived with the wine and the horse asked him: "Why are you so late with the wine?"
5. "Bah! Do you think one cannot take a little time to polish his own shoes?"

(Note: The Chilean comic strip, published in a children's magazine titled *El Volantín (The Kite),* was drawn by eleven-year-old Roberto Gonzalez for a joke by ten-year-old Maria Christina Gonzalez.)

GERMANY

The Little Centipede

The little centipede came crying to his mother: "Mommy, I have sprained my foot!"

"Which foot have you sprained, my dear?"

"I can't tell yet. I can only count to 10. . . ."

Der kleine Tausendfüssler

Der kleine Tausendfüssler kommt weinend zu seiner Mutter gelaufen: "Mutti, ich mir einen Fuss verstaucht!"

"Welchen Fuss hast du dir den verstaucht, mein Kleiner?"

"Das kann ich dir doch nicht sagen. Ich doch erst bis 10 zahlen..."

SENEGAL

When does the mouse say "Nye, nye, nye!" to the cat?
When her hole is near.

ENGLAND

What did Alfie's mother say when he came carting that twenty-foot snake out of the zoo?
"Now you go straight back and return it!"

TURKEY

One day a mosquito sat on the rough, thick-skinned neck of a water buffalo. Just then, a car passing by frightened the water buffalo, and he began running as fast as he could go.

The mosquito, surprised at the extent of her strength, came to the edge of the water buffalo's ear and said, "Brother Water Buffalo, I didn't mean to hurt you so much when I sat down. Please forgive me."

MEXICO

Why does a dog wag his tail?
Because the tail cannot wag the dog.

U.S.A.

What was the turtle doing on the road?
About half a mile an hour.

SIERRA LEONE

How Spider Sold a Big "Dog"

In Temneland one morning, Spider set out for the market. He had nothing to sell and no money, so he was not in a hurry. About halfway, he lay down beside the path and fell asleep.

Presently he woke up and saw that two men and a cow had stopped near him. He heard one of them say, "What's that thing?"

The other answered, "A big dog, ain't it?"

Spider got up and saw that they were looking at a lion stretched out on a rock sound asleep. He said, "How do."

The nearest man said, "How do. This dog here—you own him?"

"He's my very own dog," said Spider.

"He like to hunt?" asked the man.

"Hunts all the time," said Spider.

"He a good watchdog?" asked the other man.

"Nobody's gonna sneak around where he lives," said Spider.

The three palavered some more; and Spider traded his big "dog" for the cow. As he took hold of the cow's rope, he said, "Don't wake up the dog till I'm gone. Or he will follow me!" Then he hurried off, with the cow trotting behind him.

Spider sold the cow at the market and got a lot of money. But he never did hear what happened to those two stupid men when they woke up that lion.

U.S.A.

How do you keep a skunk from smelling?
Hold his nose.

▲ ▲ ▲ ▲ ▲ ▲ ▲ ▲ ▲ ▲ ▲ ▲

CZECHOSLOVAKIA

Name at least five animals living at the North Pole.
Three polar bears and two seals.

IRAN

A fisherman was taking a fish home when a friend asked, "Why didn't you sell this fine, live fish? Where are you taking him?"

The fisherman said, "I am taking it home for dinner."

Just then, the fish raised his head and said, "I've already had my dinner. You might better take me to a movie, instead!"

SOUTH AFRICA

'n Polisiebeampte stop van der Merwe wat die hoofstraat afloop met 'n krokodil op sy skouers.

"Haai, jy kan nie so rondloop met die krokodil nie. Neem dit na die dieretuin".

"Goed", kom dit gelate, "as jy so dink".

'n Paar uur later kry dieselfde beampte van der Merwe in 'n ander voorstad, nog steeds met die krokodil op sy skouers.

"Ek dag ek het jou gevra om die krokodil dieretuin toe te neem", kom die teregwysing.

"Ek het", verklaar van der Merwe. "En hy het dit so geniet dat ek hom nou fliek toe neem".

A police officer stopped van der Merwe walking down the main street with a crocodile on his shoulders.

"Hey, you can't walk around town with a crocodile like that. Take it to the zoo."

"Good," as he shrugged his shoulders, "if you say so."

A couple of hours later the same officer saw van der Merwe in a suburb, still with the crocodile on his shoulders.

"I thought I told you to take the crocodile to the zoo," he said, rushing up.

"I did," said van der Merwe. "And he enjoyed it so much now I'm taking him to the movies."

(Note: This same story is told in Argentina, but the chief character there is, of course, Jaimito.)

ITALY

Is it true that geese are gossipy?

"Me, gossipy?" the goose answered. "This is a lie the chickens must have told. Yes, sir! Three days ago, I saw them . . ."

IRAN

Doctor: My boy, didn't you notice that my office hours are from 4:00 to 8:00 P.M.? Why do you come here at 8:00 A.M.?

Boy: I noticed, Sir. But apparently the dog who bit me can't read.

SIERRA LEONE

Teacher: Tell me, who first invented underground tunnels?

Boy: Please, Sir, worms.

GERMANY

The Canary

Hans (with a cat in his arms): Miss, didn't you place an ad in the paper about a canary that flew away?

Miss: Yes, but why should I want a cat?

Hans: The canary is inside!

U.S.S.R.

Alexei: How come Comrade Ivanov's rooster always crows at exactly six o'clock, no matter what the season is?

Georgi: Well, Comrade Ivanov got tired of being awakened too early in the morning, so he bought his rooster a wristwatch!

NORWAY

En vogn kjørte hurtig på en landevei og bak vognen var det en stor støvsky. En flue som satt på vognen så seg tilbake og sa: ,,Se hvordan jeg kan hvirvle opp støv!''

A fly got on a wagon that was rapidly going down a country road stirring up a terrible cloud of dust. Said the fly: "See how I can stir up the dust!"

SPAIN

Llevo mi casa al hombro,
Camino sin una pata
y voy marcando mi huella
Con un hilito de plata.
El caracol

With my house on my shoulder,
I walk legless (funny thing!)
Tracing my footprint
With a shiny silver string.
The snail

U.S.A.

A duck, a frog, and a skunk went to a movie. Tickets cost one dollar. Which of the three got in, and which didn't?
The duck got in with its bill, the frog got in with its green back, but the skunk stayed out because it had only a (s)cent.

PHILIPPINES

There was a chick,
He was dirty, ick.
There came a hen
She was proud—ehem.
The hen saw the chick,
ick, ehem!

Bettina S. de la Fuente
Grade 2B

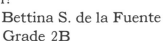

ITALY

"Why don't you play soccer, Centipede?"
"By the time I have finished tying all my shoes, the game is over!"

GREECE

The conductor on the bus asked the lady to remove her dog from the seat it was sitting on. She protested, saying that since she had paid for a ticket for the dog, the dog was entitled to a seat just like the other passengers.

"In that case, lady," he said, "just like all the other passengers, your dog must not have his feet on the seat."

NETHERLANDS ANTILLES (ARUBA)

Compa Nanzi and the Spotted Cow (a folktale)

In the land where Compa Nanzi lives—I've forgotten the name—there was a king called Shon Arey. Shon Arey owned much land, but on the largest part of this land grew a plant that pricked when you touched its leaves. After that, you started to itch wherever the plant touched you.

That kind of plant is called "bringamosa." Now I suppose you know what I mean.

With a big piece of land that has bringamosa on it, naturally you can't do very much. *That* Shon Arey understood. He wanted the land cleared, but . . .

"Well," you think, "let him get someone to work in his garden." But that wasn't so easy. I'll explain why. Shon Arey was a funny kind of king. He couldn't stand it if somebody scratched himself. The very thought—or the word "scratch"—made him itchy all over his back. That's why in his whole palace nobody was allowed to scratch himself. Whoever did it *anywhere* wasn't very happy, and he was careful not to scratch when others could see him.

But to cut out the bringamosa without touching those leaves you would have to be a magician. And there weren't any of those in the land of Shon Arey! Still, that spot of land must be cleared.

That's why the king made a proclamation: "Whoever will clear this land without scratching even once will get as a reward my beautiful milking cow."

continued

This cow was very famous because she gave the richest, tastiest milk in the land. Besides that, on Sundays and holidays she gave chocolate milk!

You can well understand that anybody would like to have a cow like that, and you'd think maybe great crowds of people would be ready to come to the king for the job. But you're wrong!

The king, who hated scratching, had said that whoever, in clearing that land, scratched himself even once would get twenty lashes. Now, you understand that nobody cared for that very much. And nobody came to the field of Shon Arey to clear it.

No one, that is, but a spider, and that spider was—you guessed it, of course—Compa Nanzi! Compa Nanzi thought, "Well, let me give it a try. I would like to have that cow." He went to the palace of the king and asked to have a word with him. Shon Arey was just taking his midday nap, and he wasn't very wide awake.

Compa Nanzi told him why he had come. Although Shon Arey was very sleepy, he was awake enough to remember that he had to beware of this trickster Compa Nanzi. He agreed that Compa Nanzi could

have the cow if he really and truly would clear that whole field. But he told him three times to be very careful not to scratch, because if he did, the king would have a soldier grab him and give him twenty lashes with his toughest stick. The clever king sent a soldier along to be sure that tricky Compa Nanzi didn't scratch.

Compa Nanzi said he understood everything, and he went with the soldier and a big spade to the land that had to be cleared. Of course, his little plan was already made. But listen! He began at once to clear away the bringamosa. The soldier sat down at the edge of the field pleased with this commission: surely Compa Nanzi was going to get what was coming to him now.

It didn't take very long before the spider began to be bothered by the prickling and itching, and—man!—he had to scratch so badly, he didn't think he could stand it. He went to the soldier, who never had finished the fifth grade in school, and he said, "Say, soldier, do you know which cow I'm going to get from the king when I've cleared this piece of land?"

The soldier laughed and said, "Hmn? You? You're never going to get a cow from the king, but you can tell me which cow you think you're going to get."

And then Compa Nanzi started: "Of course you know—that one beautiful cow with a spot here, a spot there, a spot again, a spot thus, and a spot so." And every time Compa Nanzi spoke about a spot, he pressed and rubbed his fingers hard on that spot on his body, and —of course you understand already—that was a spot where he itched.

The soldier, as I told you already, who wasn't very smart, didn't realize the trick, and just listened. And then Compa Nanzi started again: "Yes, but you know—I can't remember. Does the cow have a spot here (scratch), or does she have it there (scratch)? Oh, no, now I remember: here's where a spot is (scratch), and one there (scratch) and one here (scratch) and another one here (scratch) and another one there (scratch)." And so Compa Nanzi had a good chance to scratch all the places where the bringamosa had pricked him, without the soldier's knowing what he was really doing. In this way, he got that whole piece of land cleared without revealing that he was scratching.

The king didn't understand it at all, but he had to believe the soldier. This one told Shon Arey that Nanzi not once had scratched from being itchy.

Well, the king had to give the cow to Compa Nanzi because he had cleared his land. You understand that that smart spider also shared the wonderful red cow. Shi María (Nanzi's wife) made many of us very happy, because now they could get good, rich milk to drink, and they had wanted it very badly.

(Note: To our knowledge, this is the first time this Nanzi story has ever been translated into English from the special blend of Dutch, Spanish, Portuguese, and Indian words that is spoken only on Aruba, Bonaire, and Curaçao, a language which is called Papiamento.)

Fun with Friends

Whatʼs the quickest way to make a friend of someone? Find
something you can laugh at together. Laughter and friendship are as
natural a team as bread and spread, as necessary as water and air.

Counting-out and nonsense rhymes, ball-bouncing and rope-
jumping chants, finger and toe games, riddles, "endless" tales,
"smarty-pants" jokes, autograph-album rhymes, and droodles are
just a few of the keys that can open friendships. This chapter holds
more than seventy-five such keys, drawn from thirty-six countries in
seventeen languages besides English. Whatʼs more, these keys will
remind you of a heap more tucked away in the cupboard of your
head, keys waiting to be dusted off and used to unlock your way to
new friendships.

Does a sudden rainstorm bring you the kind of luck it brought
those two girls in Morocco? Would you like to be in there with Alfie
as he goes for a ride? How often have you hiked or jogged to "Left!
Left! I had a good home..."? Do you know any other versions of
"Ooey Gooey"? How are you on the swallow dive? and what do you
think of Mafaldaʼs system for keeping track of all her bright ideas?
(Bet youʼre glad youʼre not Felipe!)

Next time youʼre counting-out for "It," spring a new rhyme on
your friends; theyʼll all want one. (Nobody but friends will be
listening, so why not try some of the other languages, as well as your
own? Theyʼre all fun tongue-trippers.) And while youʼre at it, help
yourself to a hic-hic-hiccups cure.

If droodles are your bored-time hobby, youʼll find a whole page
of them at the end of this chapter, in four languages. Theyʼll add
variety to the notes you pass to your friends. Where? In *school?*
Hmmnn...

SWEDEN

Sven: My mother's father grew up on one of the skerries (islands) near Norrtälje, so he had to get a loan when he went to the university. He studied five years there, and do you know what? He's still paying off his student loan, though he finished his schooling at Lund twenty-two years ago.

Per: That's nothing. Birgitta says that her father's father grew up in the Northland and went *eight* years to the university. He had a student loan, too, of course, and when the old man died, her father had to finish paying off her grandfather's student loan before the estate could be settled!

(Since education is considered very important in Sweden, any serious upper-level student can borrow money from the State to finish his schooling; the student loans, without security and even without interest during the first two years, can be repaid over a period of ten or fifteen years. This Swedish joke is pure exaggeration.)

VIETNAM

Two young boys are bragging about their fathers.

"My father is a marine captain. Many people fear and obey him."

"Ouf! That's nothing. My father can even give an order to the President to bow his head and sit still."

"Really? Who is he?"

"He's a barber!"

BELGIUM

What is the difference between an elephant and a flea?
The elephant can have fleas but the flea can't have elephants.

Quelle est la différence entre un éléphant et une puce?
L'éléphant peut avoir des puces mais la puce ne peut pas avoir d'éléphant.

MOROCCO

Pluie

Les deux fillettes se promènent, suivies de la mère de l'une d'elles. Au bout d'un moment, il commence à tomber quelques gouttes. Alors, une des petites:

—Chic, il va pleuvoir.

—Tu aimes la pluie tant cela? S'informe sa petite copine.

—Non, mais en général, quand il pleut, maman nous emmène nous mettre a l'abri chez le pâtissier.

Rain

Two young girls were walking, followed by the mother of one of them. After a moment, some raindrops began to fall.

"Great! It's going to rain," exclaimed the woman's daughter.

"You like the rain that much," her friend asked curiously.

"No," the daughter replied, "but generally, when it rains, Mama finds shelter for us at a pastry shop."

JAMAICA

"What's the difference between lightning and electricity?"

"I don't know. What is?"

"Lightning's free!"

ENGLAND

Mum (to boys playing with a huge snowball): Have you boys seen my son Alfie?

George: Yes, ma'am. We're giving your Alfie a ride. He's inside this snowball!

MEXICO

I hunted up a cobbler
For to make me a pair of
    shoeses,
With the toes all nicely rounded
Like a duck's bill or a goose's.
Confound that wretched
    cobbler,
How he fooled me, though!
He made me up the shoeses,
But not the duck-bill toe!

(A popular playground song)

ARGENTINA

"Take it! . . . And let's see when
you'll learn to write!"
"Thank you, Philip."

"What did Philip write for you
on that paper?"
"One of the things I have to
do during my life."

"Since I don't want to forget all
of the things I have to do during
my lifetime, as soon as they
occur to me I ask Philip to write
them down."
"And that makes him angry?"

"Yes."

(Note: This is one of countless "Mafalda" strips,
popular throughout Latin America.)

Fingers and feet are sources of fun around the world. On this and the following pages you'll find a double fistful of the thousands of games and rhymes and riddles and tricks that take advantage of these handy appendages.

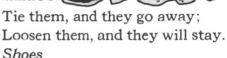

MEXICO

This one stole an egg;
This one fried it;
This one put salt on it;
This one ate it;
And this old dog went and told
    all about it!

U.S.A.

What has a thousand legs and
    can't walk?
Five hundred pairs of pants

MEXICO

Tie them, and they go away;
Loosen them, and they will stay.
Shoes

SAUDI ARABIA

(Little finger) Saghear wa aagill,
(Ring finger) Lubbass alkhawatim,
(Middle finger) Labeer wa majjnoon,
(Index finger) Lahass algodour,
(Thumb) Gassaa algomoul
(Let index finger and middle finger
  run up child's arm) Fain abat, fain abat,
(Tickle child in armpit) Tahat albatt.

Young and wise,
The ring wearer,
Old and crazy,
The pan licker,
The flea-killer,
Where I'm going to spend the night,
  where I'm going to spend the night,
Under the arm.

ZAÏRE

(Little finger) Oso l ô njala!	I'm hungry!
(Ring finger) 'Na ófótolámbélé ndé?	Why don't you cook for us?
(Middle finger) An' ĕl' ísó ŏtoleki botálé ná?	Among us, who is the largest?
(Index finger) Tóky'ă njala, t'ôkita nd' êtálé?	We were talking about hunger.
(Thumb, with scorn) Lonjil'em njîmane nd'	Is it now about length?
âdala bakinyo.	Wait. I'll leave your jabbering.

(Note: Among the Nkundo of Zaïre, this finger game explains why the thumb is separated from the rest of the fingers. The children choose to see the thumb as the grown-up who withdraws himself because he cannot stand the children's questions and their chatter.)

SPAIN

Aquest és el pare,	This one is the papa,
Aquesta és la mare,	This one is the mama,
Aquest fa les sopes,	This one cooks the soup,
Aquest se les menja totes.	This one gobbles it up.
I aquest diu: piu, piu, piu!	And this one says, "Piu, piu, piu!
Que no n'hi ha pel caganiu?	Is there nothing for the smallest one, too?"

NEW ZEALAND

Boy: Doctor, will I be able to
   play the violin after this
   cast comes off my wrist?
Doctor: Certainly, my son.
Boy: Wonderful! I've never
   been able to play the violin
   before.

SYRIA

A little boy hurried into a
cosmetics shop and asked,
"Lady, do you have fingernails?"

"Yes, of course," she replied.

"Then please scratch my back
right here. I have a flea bite
that I can't reach!"

AFGHANISTAN

It walked and walked
And walked all day;
Home at night
It came to stay.
Totally tired
From that long way,
With its mouth open,
On the floor it lay.
A shoe

AUSTRALIA

Peanut sitting on a railway
   track;
Its heart was all a-flutter.
An engine came around the
   curve—
(Whistle) Peanut butter!

CHILE

De día llenos de carne,
y por la noche
llenos de aire.
Los zapatos

———————

By day full of meat,
and by night
full of air.
Shoes

AUSTRALIA

Ooey Gooey was a worm;
A little worm was he.
He sat upon the railway
track;
The train he did not see.
The train came roaring
round the bend.
The driver blew his squeal;
He came out with his
pocket knife
And scraped him off the
wheel.
Ooey gooey.

U.S.A.

Left! Left!
I had a good home and I
left.
I left my wife and sixteen
guinea pigs.
Hay foot! Straw foot!
Gotta get the *right* foot.
Left! Left!
I had a good home and I
left.
I left my wife . . .
(and on and *on*: a chant
that's used in Scout camps
on hikes, among many other
places.)

GERMANY

Maxie: Guess, now. When
    the head of a cow points
    north, where will her tail
    point?
Hans: To the south,
    naturally!
Maxie: Not at all naturally.
    It points to the ground, as
    usual.

SIERRA LEONE

Alex: Ken, can you do a
    swallow dive?
Ken: It's quite easy. Just dive
    into the pool and swallow
    up the water!

TOOT
TOOT

CANADA

Bob: Our dog is just like one of the family.

Joe: Which one?

PANAMA

—Que es lo que tiene tres pies pero no puede caminar?

—*Una yarda.*

What has three feet but cannot walk?

A yard

AUSTRIA

"Why is your little brother crying?"

"He fell down."

"Where?"

"On the backside of his belly!"

GUYANA

Tom: David, why did your father choose a bicycle instead of a cow when he won first prize at the raffle?

David: Well, he thought he'd look silly trying to ride a cow to market.

Tom: And how will he look if he tries to milk a bicycle?

Do you ever get tired of using the same old counting-out and nonsense rhymes? Well, try a few of *these*, for a change!

SWEDEN

Åla, dåla;
Fike, fake;
Bande, kråke;
Stina, stana;
Bus, bas;
Knis, knas;
Knagen.

(Note: *Bande* means "farmer"; *krake* means "blackbird"; Stina is a person's name; the rest are nonsense sounds.)

Apala, mesala,
Mesinko, meso,
Sebedei, sebedo;
Extra, lara,
Kajsa, Sara!
Heck, veck,
Vällingseck,
Gack du din långe man veck,
Ut!

(Note: The last two lines *do* make sense:
Man, go your length away, Out!)

GERMANY

Anege, hanige,
Serege, strige,
Ripeti, pipeti, Knoll.

GERMANY

Ona, bona,
Tanta, rona,
Ita, bita, bonn.

ESTONIAN

Essike, tessike,
Tonko, lonko,
Simike, mâke,
Kulte, kalte,
Mâkama, tais,
Tilleri, tippan, tuttan, pois.

(Note: *Pois* means "out.")

POLAND

Ene, due, ryke, fake,
Torba, borba, ósme, smake.
Eus, deus, kosmateus,
Baks!

———————

Ene, due, ryke, fake,
Bag, borba, eight, smake.
Eus, deus, kosmateus,
Baks!

(Note: Most of these are nonsense words.)

NETHERLANDS

Eeze, weeze, wes.
Olie in het vlees;
Olie in de kan.
Wie is de man?

———————

Eeze, weeze, wes.
Oil in the flesh;
Oil in the can.
Who is the man?

(Note: Eeze, weeze, wes are nonsense sounds.)

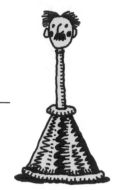

MADAGASCAR

Isa ny amontana
Roa ny aviavy
Telo fangady
Efa drofia
Dimy emboka
Eni mangamanga
Fito paraky
Valo tanantanana
Sivy rongony
Folo fànoléhana

———————

One, the amontana (tree)
Two, the aviavy (trees)
Three, spades
Four, sofia (palms)
Five, gums
Six, blues
Seven, tobacco
Eight, gourds
Nine, hemp
Ten, fanolehana (get out)

If the rhymes on pages 79 and 80 weren't enough to give you a taste of round-the-world getting-ready fun, here's a bonus of a few more, with some new rhymes for ball-bouncing, rope-jumping, and see-sawing to change the sound on the playground.

MEXICO

Al subir una montaña
Una pulga me picó;
La cogí de las narices
Y se me escapó.
Botín, botero, y salió.
Rosa, clavel, y botón.

On climbing a mountain
A flea bit me;
I caught it by the nose
And it escaped from me.
Botín, botero, and away went he.
Rose, carnation, and bud.

NETHERLANDS

Zagen, zagen, wille wille wage;
Jan kwam thuis een boterham vrage.
Vader was niet thuis;
Moeder was niet thuis;
"Piep" zei de muis in het zomerhuis.

Sawing, sawing, wheels wheels
    wagging;
John came home a sandwich
    begging.
Father was not at the house;
Mother was not at the house;
"Peep," said the mouse in its
    summerhouse.

U.S.A.

My mama and your mama
Live across the way.
Every night they have a fight
And this is what they say:
Acka backa soda cracka
Acka backa boo
Acka backa soda cracka
Out goes you!

NIGERIA

Iyòo, ó
Abo, kwekwe,
ihwu, Iruka
ede
bwaloka, okabwalede,
ńkpi bwaloka.

――――――

Oh, oh, oh, oh
Girls, agree,
tall girl, Iruka
koko yams
sour sour koko yams,
he goat sour.

(Note: This rhyme, translated word for word,
is a pure nonsense combination of other words.)

CANADA

One, two, three, four, five, six,
    seven,
All good children go to heaven.
Those who swear don't go there.
One, two, three, four, five, six,
    seven.

CANADA

All in together, girls!
This fine weather, girls!
I saw the preacher kiss the
    teacher.
How many kisses did he give
    her?
1, 2, 3, 4, 5 . . .

AUSTRALIA

Up the Mississippi,
If you miss a loop you're
    out-i-o;
If you had been where I have
    been
You wouldn't have been put
    out-i-o.

(A skipper who misses her loop, or jump,
has to take one end of the rope and turn.)

IRELAND

Long-legged Italy kicked poor
    Sicily into the
    Mediterranean Sea.
Russia was Hungary, so she ate
    a piece of Turkey dipped in
    Greece.
Ireland, England, Scotland,
    Wales are all tied up in
    donkeys' tails!

(A play on countries' names used as a jump-
rope rhyme.)

You *still* haven't found a rhyme that's better than your old one?
Well, here's another go-around. But three means O-U-T . . .

NETHERLANDS

Eun, deun, dip;
Volle, kale, kip;
Volle, kale, mosterd halen;
Eun, deun, dip.

Eun, deun, dip;
Full, bald chicken;
Full, bald, go and get the
    mustard;
Eun, deun, dip.

(Note: Eun, deun, dip are nonsense sounds.)

SWITZERLAND

Ene, dene, Dintenfass,
Geh' in d' Schul' und lerne was;
Wenn du was gelernet hast,
Kommst du heim und sagst mir das.
Eins, zwei, drei,
Du bist frei!

Ene, dene, bottle of ink,
Go to school and learn
    something.
When you have learned
    something,
Come home and tell it to me.
One two, three,
You are free!

SCOTLAND

Tit, tat, toe,
Here I go,
And if I miss
I pitch on this.

FINLAND

Maalari maalas
Taloa sinistä ja.
Punaista illan tullen
Sanoi hän nyt mä
Lähden pelistä pois.

A painter painted a house
Blue and red.
When evening came he said
Now I'll go
From this game *out*.

INDIA

Atakan, patakan bawan bichawā,
Khombadi, know, dir khaw,
Han mat ghodā, tāyam, tûyam,
Sut, luk, but, luk.

(Note: This bit of doggerel uses several
words that have meaning in present-
day India and others purely for sound
and for fun. *Patakan is* "immediately,"
bawan is "fifty-two," *bichawā* is
"chicken," *han mat ghodā* is a particular kind of horse, and *tāyam,
tûyam* is the sound made by the
prancing of a skittish horse; the last
line includes rhyming sounds that are
pure nonsense.)

ANDORRA

Chirrichti, mirrichti, gerrena, plat, olio, zopa, kikili, salda, hurrup, edo klik!

(Most of these are nonsense sounds and can not be translated; at the end are these words: "roll," "plate," "oil," "soup," and "bouillon.")

▶▶▶▶▶▶▶▶▶▶▶▶▶▶▶▶▶▶▶▶▶▶▶▶▶▶▶▶▶▶

Got the hic-hic-hiccups? One or the other of these Dutch hiccups-go-way charms may do the trick!

NETHERLANDS

Ik heb de hik;
Ik heb de slik.
Ik heb hem nu en ik heb hem dan.
Geef hem aan een andere man,
Die hem goed verdragen kan.
(and a slightly different version)
Hik sprik, sprouw,
Ik geef de hik aan Jan.
Geef de hik aan een anderer man,
Die de hik verdragen kan.

———————

I have the hiccups;
I have the slickups.
I have them now and I have
    them again.
Give them to another man
Who will handle them the best
    he can.
(and a slightly different version)
Hic (and two words for sound),
I give the hiccups to Jan.
Give the hiccups to another man,
Who will handle the hiccups the
    best he can.

CUBA

Tin marín	(nonsense sounds)
de dos Pingües;	(of two Pingües;)
cúcara macara	(nonsense sounds)
títere fue!	(nonsense sounds)
Pasó la mula;	(The mule went by;)
pasó Miguel.	(Miguel went by)
Mira a ver	(Look and see)
quien fue!	(who it was.)
No me pínches	(Do not poke me)
con cuchillo;	(with the knife;)
pínchame	(poke me)
con tenedor.	(with the fork.)

(Note: The last three words of the Spanish are directed to five different children, each poked in turn by the one counting, on "Pínchame/con/ten/e/dor.")

SWEDEN

Essike, tessike,
Sômer mâker,
Dicker dacker,
Kilter kalter,
Waggam walter,
Tippan tillan, pois.
(Note: *Pois* means "out.")
(and O-U-T for
me . . .)

Autograph albums—fancy ones and ones made just of folded
notebook paper—can be found around the world, and new rhymes
and old ones rub shoulders with one another from page to page. Can
you find some new ones here from some other country to add flavor
to the fun you have with your friends' autograph albums?

TURKEY

Şair değilim şiir yazayim.
Ressam değilim resim yapayim,
Şu kötü yazimla bir imza atayim.

I'm not a poet with poems that
   flow.
I'm not a painter, with pictures
   to show,
So only my name, ugly scrawl,
   is below.

U.S.A.

DEAR HELEN,
I 🚗 CRY
I 🚗 LAUGH
I 🚗 SIGN
YOUR 🚗 GRAPH
🚗 = AUTO   JACKIE D.
GOOD LUCK!

SCOTLAND

Remember M
Remember E
Put them together
And remember ME.

MEXICO

A-E-I-O-U—
El burro sabe
Más que tú.

A-E-I-O-U—
The burro, too,
Knows more than you.

CANADA

Just plant a watermelon on my
   grave,
And let the juice slurp through.
Just plant a watermelon on my
   grave:
That's all I ask of you.
Fresh fried chicken is mighty
   fine,
But all I ask is a melon on the
   vine.
Just plant a watermelon on my
   grave,
And let the juice slurp through!

AUSTRALIA

You asked me for an autograph,
   Just a word or two,
But being in a generous mood
   I've given you twenty-two.

Did you ever tell your friends an "endless tale"? If so, you have company in that kind of fun all around the world. Here are some samples to get you started.

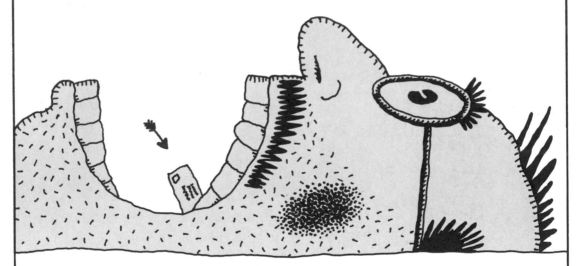

SWITZERLAND

Once there was a man who had a hole in his tooth. In this hole there was a little box into which he was putting a letter in which was written, "Once there was a man who had a hole in his tooth. In this hole there was a little box into which he was putting a letter in which was written, 'Once there was a man . . .' "

(and the "story" goes on until a friend cries, "STOP IT!")

IRELAND

One day the Fianna went west over the hill and then they came back east over the hill and then they went west over the hill and then they came back east over the hill and then they went west over the hill and then they came back east . . .

(until someone shouts, "For crying out loud, get them out of the hill!")

MEXICO

Once upon a time there was a cat
With a little rag tail
And eyes wrong-side out.
Do you want me to tell it again?
    (repeated endlessly)

U.S.A.

I laughed so hard I thought I'd
    die. I did die.
They buried me, and a flower
    grew on my grave.
The roots grew down and tickled
    me. I laughed so hard I
    thought I'd die. I did die. . . .
    (repeated endlessly until
somebody cries, "Stop!")

U.S.A.

Wanna hear my story?
Well,
My boyfriend's name was
Fatty—
He came from Cincinnati,
With a pimple on his nose
and ten fat toes,
And this is how my story goes:
My mother was born in
England;
My father was born in
France,
And I was born in diapers
Because I had no pants.
Oh, you wanna hear my
story? Well, . . .

ENGLAND

It was a dark and stormy night;
the rain came down in torrents;
there were brigands in the
mountains, and thieves; and the
chief said to Antonio, "Antonio,
tell us a story." And Antonio, in
fear and dread of the mighty
chief, began his story: "It was a
dark and stormy night; the rain
came down in torrents; there
were brigands . . . "
    (and on and on and on . . .)

These droodles appeared in Switzerland on a railroad giveaway for children, in four different languages. Can you read all four? Can you droodle some more?

Reject from pretzel factory
Brezel (fehlerhaftes Stuck)
Ciambella difettosa
Bretzel raté

Lipstick left on boar's neck
Lippenstiftabdruck am Hals eines männlichen Landschweines
Traccia di rossetto sul collo di un porco di campagna
Marque de rouge à lèvres sur le cou d'un porc des champs

Baby pacifier for twins
Baby-Schnuller für Zwillinge
Succhietto per gemelli
Sucette pour jumeaux

Suspicious pig watching electrical wall socket
Schwein, argwohnisch eine Steckdose betrachtend
Maiale sospettoso, che osserva una presa di corrente
Porc considerant une prise électrique d'un air soupçonneux

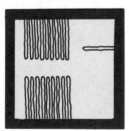

Worm General inspecting his troops
Regenwurmgeneral nimmt eine Parade ab
Parata di lombrichi davanti al loro generale
Le général des lombrics à la parade

Toothbrush for toothless person
Zahnbürste eines Zahnlosen
Spazzolino per pulire i denti di uno sdentato
Brosse à dents d'un édenté

Tricks and Teases

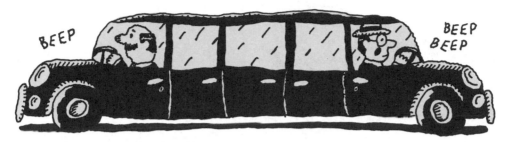

BEEP   BEEP BEEP

Half of the fun in having a friend is being able to *tease* that friend and still keep the friendship strong. From all six continents—from forty-five countries ranging from Afghanistan to Zambia in twenty-four languages plus English—have come jokes and riddles and tales and "snappers" galore, all meant for sharing and shouting about.

Did you know that the egg is the subject of more riddles around the world than is any other item? On pages 103 and 104, you'll find a whole omelet of egg riddles. (If your friends are allergic to eggs, there's a bumper crop of other kinds of riddles stored throughout this book.) And how nimble is your tongue? Try wrapping it around one of the tangle tongue twisters on pages 97 and 98—yes, the original as well as the English translation!—and then challenge a friend to do the same stunt.

Have you met the Rock-eating Dragon? Have you ever driven a better bargain for half a watermelon than Hasan did? Does a goblin live in your house? Have you ever fast-talked your way into the movies with the kind of "wrinkle" used in South Africa? And has one of your tricks ever backfired the way Barbu's did?

Here you'll find both the tricksters and the tricked. Don't worry about van der Merwe, but keep a sharp eye out for both Andare and Sly Peter...and any of those *andiyas*. Watermelon Rind, a favorite character among Chinese-speaking children, loses one in this chapter; many times, he's the winner. A word of caution: Don't bend over in Panama!

Thus armed, you'll be well prepared both to deliver and to receive a whole bundle of tricks and teases.

IRAN

اولی — معذرت می خواهم آقا ساعت چنده ؟

دومی — لطفاً ساکت شوید خوابیده ·

(Read the Persian from right to left.)

The First One: Pardon me. What does your watch say?
The Second One: Please be quiet. It has gone to sleep.

(Note: The telling of time is handled in one of two ways in Persian, or Farsi: In terms of "How much is the watch?"—to which a natural joking answer is "It's pretty expensive!"—or in terms of "How is the watch?" to which the above would be a joking response in indication that the watch had stopped.) Rarinih Baf supplied this joke for a magazine *Rainbow* edited by 11-year-old Neema Mir-Montahari.

AFGHANISTAN

In a garden of many a
    blossoming tree,
A dewy beauty I see,
Seated on her father's knee.
"Give," say I, "a kiss to me."
"Today not a chance," says she.
"Not even tomorrow can that be.
The day after that, perhaps I'll
    agree
That you kiss, smack your lips,
and be free
    With me."
  A sour orange.

Note: This riddle is thought in bad taste by adults but is very popular among boys in Afghanistan.

TAIWAN

("Watermelon Rind" is the children's favorite in the Sunday edition of the CHINA DAILY, in Taiwan. Read from top to bottom and right to left.)

Title: Watermelon Rind
(the name of the boy with the striped shirt)

1. "Watermelon Rind, you work really fast!"
2. "Oh, look! The sun is so strong and bright!" (While Watermelon Rind looks, his friend throws his own socks into the wash.)
3. "Gee. That's funny. I didn't remember I had a pair of black socks."
4. "Oh, they're not quite dry. I'll be back for them later." "So I washed his socks again!"

NIGERIA

What will you get if you join 3/5 of a chick to 2/3 of a cat and to 1/2 of a goat?

Chicago.

THAILAND

Mr. A.: Hey, did we have a heavy rain yesterday?

Mr. B.: How do I know? I didn't weigh it!

PANAMA

"En tiempo de guerra uno no se agacha."

"In wartime, one does not bend over."

(Note: This is said in Panama when you catch someone bending over and you give him a little kick in the rear, as a prank.)

AUSTRALIA

Did you hear the joke about the butter?

Good—don't spread it!

NORWAY

En mann, som bodde i et hus hvor en nisse hadde slått seg til, klarte ikke å bli kvitt nissen. En dag bestemte han seg til a flytte og la nissen få huset. Da mannen komm ut med det siste han eidde, satt nissen på toppen av lasset og lo: "Så vi har flyttedag i dag vi to!"

———————

A man who lived in a house where a goblin had chosen to dwell decided he would move out and let the goblin have it. He had taken several loads of his goods away and was taking his last load, which was mainly empty boxes and other rubbish. Then, by chance, he discovered the goblin sitting in an empty box. With the whole move thus in vain, he became very angry, but the goblin laughed heartily as he stuck his head up out of the box and said, "It seems we two are moving today!"

FRANCE

Little boy, coming up to a little girl huddled with her sheep under a tree during a rainstorm:

"You ought to take your sheep in. You know wool shrinks in the wash!"

SOUTH AFRICA

Van der Merwe was on his way to England when the ship sank. He
found himself sharing a thick plank with McTavish. Between them
they had no food and water except a small piece of *biltong*. There
was a heated dispute over the *biltong* until the two decided that the
smarter man of the two would have it. To settle this point, they were
to take the meat in their teeth, one at each end. Whoever held it
longer in his teeth would get it. Both men bit hard. "Reet?" inquired
McTavish. "Ja," said van der Merwe—and lost the *biltong*!

(*Biltong* is a dried meat like beef jerky. *Reet,* meaning "right" in Afrikaans, is said with the
teeth closed; *ja*, meaning "yes" In Afrikaans, is said *yah* and with the mouth open.)

INDIA

A kind-hearted gentleman was
passing by when he saw a small
boy trying to reach a doorbell.

   "Here, Sonny," he said. "I'll
ring it for you. Now, is there
anything else I can do for you?"

   "Just run as fast as you can,"
said the little boy. "That's what
I'm going to do, Mister!"

INDONESIA

Hasan: How much is this
   watermelon?
Fruit Seller: One hundred
   Rupiah each.
Hasan: Oh, that is expensive.
Fruit Seller: You can buy
   only a half for sixty Rupiah.
Hasan: O.K. I'll take the
   other half for forty Rupiah.

(Note: There are 420 Rupiah to $1.)

MEXICO

What is necessary to light a
candle?
The candle.

PORTUGAL

An elegant lady,
Of fine ladies queen,
Dressed all in silks,
With just rags to be seen.
A hen.

(Note: The "rags" are the silky ends of the
   hen's feathers.)

SRI LANKA

Seven wandering *andiyas* (beggars) once happened to spend the night at the same *ambalama* (resting place). They agreed to cook a common pot of *congee* (rice cooked in hot water) for their dinner, with each *andiya* contributing a handful of rice.

One by one, each *andiya* reached out over the pot to drop in his rice. But—tricky fellows that they were—none of them put a single grain into the pot. Each beggar thought the others would provide the promised handful.

When the *congee* was served, each *andiya* received a bowlful of hot water!

(Note: This tale is so well known in Sri Lanka that it has become the basis for a proverb: "As the *andiyas* cooked *congee.*")

AUSTRALIA

"What do you get if you cross a tiger with a parrot?"
"I don't know, but when it talks you listen!"

PANAMA

There were six men under a single small umbrella. Why didn't any of them get wet?
It wasn't raining.

SWAZILAND

Ngikuphica ngemasotsha ami latsi angahlasela afe.
Imphendvulo: Tintsi temetshiso.

———

I have soldiers who, after attacking or firing, die.
Unused matches.

TURKEY

Şekere benzer—tadi yok;
Gökte uçar—kanadi yok.
Kar.

———

Looks like sugar—sweet is not;
Flies in the air—no wings has got.
Snow.

NICARAGUA

Primero se pregunta: "¿Cómo se llama un dragón que vive en el centro de la tierra y que come piedras?"

Después de que otra persona haya tratado de adivinar el nombre, se le dice que se llama "Dragón Que Come Piedras."

Entonces se pregunta otra vez: "¿Que pasaría si se abriera un hoyo que, pasando por el centro, fuera de un lado al otro lado del mundo, y se tirara una piedra por el hoyo?"

Después de la respuesta de la otra persona (que probablemente sea que la piedra sale por el otro lado), se le dice que está equivocada, que la piedra no sale por el otro lado . . . porque el dragón siempre se la come.

First one to the second one: "What do you call a dragon that sits in the middle of the earth eating rocks?"

After the other person has thought hard to guess the name, he is told that it is called "A Rock-eating Dragon."

Then the second one is asked: "Now, what would happen if you drilled a hole that, passing through the center, came out on the other side of the earth, and you dropped a rock through the hole?"

After getting from the other person the answer (that probably the rock would fall out the other side), he is told that he's wrong: that the rock wouldn't come out on the other side . . . because the dragon would eat it.

(Note: This joke is so well known in Nicaragua that a recent best-selling novel published there carried the title *The Last of the Rock-eating Dragon.*)

SOUTH AFRICA

Little Boy: Can you please give me thirty cents so that I can go to my parents?

Man: Certainly, boy. Here is thirty cents. But where are your parents?

Little Boy: At the movies, Sir.

NORWAY

"Do you know why our cow wears a bell?"

"No. Why?"

"Because her horns won't work!"

CANADA

Nabuchodonosor était roi de Babylon; écrivez cela en 4 lettres. *Cela.*

_____

Nebuchadnezzar was the king of Babylon; write that in 4 letters. *THAT*.

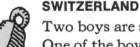

SWITZERLAND

Two boys are sitting at a table. One of the boy divides a sausage into two pieces, one very small and one very big. He gives the little one to his friend and keeps the big one for himself.

"Why did you give me the small one?" asks his friend.

The boy answers quickly, "I divided it the way you do. When you divide you always give me the big one."

SRI LANKA

That tricky Andare saw a man come to collect toddy from a certain *kitul* tree every morning. "I'll just see how that toddy tastes," Andare decided. And very early the next morning he climbed the *kitul* tree, carrying a sickle in his hand. Ah, but the drink was delicious!

Suddenly the owner came. Calmly Andare climbed down the tree, still carrying his sickle.

"What were you doing in my tree?"

"As you can see from the sickle in my hand, I was trying to cut some grass for my cow."

"But grass doesn't grow high up in a *kitul* tree!" exclaimed the owner.

"You are right," agreed Andare. "That's why I came back down." And off he went, full of toddy.

(Note: Toddy is a sweet sap from any one of various East Indian palm trees and used as a beverage; it can also be fermented to make an intoxicating drink. Andare is well known in Sri Lanka for his pranks.)

BULGARIA

What did the porcupine say as he passed a cactus plant in the botanical garden?
Hello, Cousin.

U.S.A.

Teacher: Order, children! Order!
Smarty: O.K. I'll have chocolate.

Try twisting thy tongue through these tongue-tanglers!

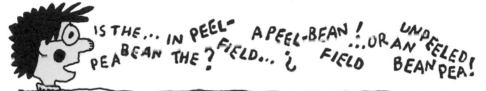

NIGERIA

Ọmọ dúdú da ọdà dudu sórí eedú dúdú.

The black child pours black paint on the black charcoal.

Iyan mu ire yọ; iyan ro ire ru.

When famine's familiar the cricket's delicious;
when famine's finished, the cricket's banished.

KOREA

들의 콩깍지 깐 콩깍지인가, 안 깐 콩깍지인가?

Is the pea-bean in the peel in the field a peeled pea-bean or an unpeeled pea-bean?

SWITZERLAND

Dää Hansdampf im Schnäggeloch hät alläs was är wiill. Und was är wiill das hät är nööd und was är hät das wiill är nööd. Dää Hansdampf im Schnäggeloch...

John in the snailhouse has all that he will. And what he wants he has not and what he has he wants not. John in the snailhouse . . .

TURKEY

Bir berber bir berbere bre berber bir berber dükkânı açalım demis. Hiç.
Bir berber bir berbere bir berber dükkânı açalım der mi?

One barber to another barber, Hey, barber, let's open a barbershop.
Bah! Does one barber ever say to another barber, Let's open a
barbershop together?

NIGER

Nde diwa, ndu dunya; ndu diwa, nde dunya; nde diwa, ndu dunya; ndu diwa,
nde dunya . . .

She jumped, he ducked; he jumped, she ducked; she jumped, he
ducked; he jumped, she ducked . . .

ENGLAND

How many cans can a cannibal nibble, if a cannibal can nibble cans?

U.S.A.

How much wood would a
woodchuck chuck if a
woodchuck could chuck wood?
As much wood as a woodchuck
should chuck if a woodchuck
could chuck wood.

ITALY

Pio pesta il pepe
al Papa; il Papa pesta il pepe a Pio.

Pio pounds pepper for the Pope;
the Pope pounds pepper for Pio.

CHINESE

屋	嘴	鹿	宿
UK	DUK	LUK	SUK
HOUSE	REAR	DEER	SLEEP

At the house rear sleeps the deer.

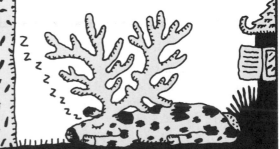

SWEDEN

First Come, First Served . . .

One day before trains and cars were invented, a peasant hired the last pair of fresh horses from a post station. He was about to drive away when up dashed a high-class carriage with footmen and liveried coachman. "See here," said the fine gentleman in the carriage. "I'm in a great hurry. Let *me* hire those horses, and you wait for yours until the next lot of fresh horses is brought."

The peasant just shook his head.

"What! You *refuse?* Do you know who I am? I'm the Governor!" said the gentleman.

"Your Honor," said the peasant, "do you know who *I* am?"

"No," said the Governor scornfully.

"Well, I'm the man who got here first and ordered these horses." And away he drove!

BULGARIA

The Nightingale and the Turkey

One day in the marketplace Sly Peter had a fine fat turkey to sell. Next to him stood Nasrudin, with a tiny nightingale perched in a cage and singing most hauntingly. Yes, Nasrudin planned to sell his nightingale. . . .

Along came a customer. "My, but that bird certainly can sing! How much are you asking for it?"

"Half a gold coin," the owner answered.

"Hmnn . . . not a bad price for such a fine voice," the customer said.

"But have you noticed my fine fat turkey?" asked Sly Peter, not to be outdone.

At that, the customer looked the turkey over. It was indeed a handsome fowl, well feathered, and certain to make several good meals. "And how much are you asking for it?"

"Five gold coins," said Sly Peter firmly.

"Five gold coins!" exclaimed the customer. "Why, that's ten times the price of that sweet-voiced nightingale!"

"Sir," said Sly Peter, determined to make the sale. "To compare a turkey with a nightingale is as difficult as to compare a fine fat watermelon with a fig. Still, if comparisons must be made, I might remind you that my turkey is far more than ten times the size and weight of that nightingale."

"Ah, but the voice of the nightingale is so beautiful," said Nasrudin, "that one might well forget that difference in weight."

"Aha!" retorted Sly Peter. "I'm happy you mentioned the voice again. That is the other great advantage of my turkey over Nasrudin's: he is quiet. Have you forgotten that speech is silver, but silence is golden?"

And with that wise remark, Sly Peter made the sale.

(Note: Nasrudin, Sly Peter's competitor on this and other occasions in Bulgarian folk tradition, is known in Turkey as Nasreddin Hoca and is himself a very clever fellow. May the better man win.)

AFGHANISTAN

معاينه يك طبيب

شخصى پيش طبيب رفت و گفت دلم درد ميكند طبيب گفت : چه خورده‌اى گفت :

نان سوخته ، طبيب چشم اورا معاينه كرد و خواست به چشم آن دوا ريزد آنشخص

گفت : طبيب صاحب چشم درد نمى كند دلم درد ميكند • طبيب گفت : اگر چشمت سالم

(Read from right to left.)

ميبود نان سوخته راميديدى و نمى خوردى •

ارسالى : محمد صابر لمحه

Check-up by Physician

A man went to a physician and said that he had a stomachache. The physician asked, "What have you eaten?"

The man said, "Burnt bread."

The physician examined his eyes and was just about to drop some medicine into them when the man said, "Sir, my eyes are not aching; my stomach is aching."

The physician said "If your eyes were healthy, you would have seen that the bread was burnt, and you wouldn't have eaten it."

—Mohammed Saber Lahmeh

MALTA

Insakkra go fik
U jistghu jisiquhielek.
Qalb.

_____

Locked inside you, yet it can be taken away from you.
Heart.

CHAD

What is it that even the ostrich with its long neck and sharp eyes cannot see?
What will happen tomorrow.

ZIMBABWE

Black cattle which stay in a forest.
Lice.

PHILIPPINES

Hugis puso, kulay ginto.
Mangga.

_____

Its shape a heart, its color gold.
Mango.

INDONESIA

Orang Tinggi

Amat: 'Mit, kemarin aku me lihat anak kira² tingginja ada 3 meter. Padahal dia masih berumur 10 tahun!
Amit: Wah...anak adjaib kalau begitu!
Amat: Bukan kok anak biasa. Hanja dia naik egrang (Djangkungan)
Amit: Oh...kukira.

_____

Cory-Kediri

A Tall One

Amat: 'Mit, yesterday I saw a child about ten feet high. And what's more, he was only ten years old!
Amit: Wow! That must be a weird child!
Amat: No, no. It was a normal child—only he was up in a tree.
Amit: Oh . . . nuts to you.

(Note: In Indonesia, friends create nicknames for each other by using only the last syllable of the name: *Amit* becomes *'Mit,* and *Kakak* becomes *'Kak.* This joke involves a play on words: tinggi means "tall" when one is speaking of people, but it can also mean "high" or "elevated.")

Riddles about eggs roll around the world . . .

PERU

Imasmari imasmari? Iskay mikhuna kashan huh mankapi. Imata chay?
Runtu. _____

There is something; there is something?
In a pot there are two kinds of food. What is it?
An egg.

MALAWI

I have built my house without any door.
An egg.

ZAMBIA

Guess the riddle:
A little house absolutely entire? Has it a door?
An egg.

TURKEY

Bir fıçım var,
İçinde iki türlü suyum var.
Yumurta. _____

I have a barrel, thin as thin,
With two kinds of water in.
An egg.

U.S.A.

A white house full of meat,
But no door to go in to eat.
An egg.

PORTUGAL

Sou filho de pais cantantes,
minha mãe não tinha dentes,
nem nenhum dos meus parentes;
eu de mim todo sou calvo,
meu coração e amarelo,
e o meu rosto é alvo e belo.
O ovo. _____

Of singing fathers I'm a son,
Of teeth my mother has not one,
My relatives have also none;
Poor me, I'm bald as I can be,
There's a yellow heart inside of me,
My fair white face is all you see.
The egg.

ZIMBABWE

Let us swap riddles:
The huge pot without an opening.
An egg.

PANAMA

Blanco como las nubes;
Amarillo como el sol;
Si me caigo me rompo.
Qué soy?
Un huevo. _____

White as the clouds;
Yellow as the sun;
If I fall I break.
What am I?
An egg.

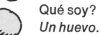

JAMAICA

What is more useful
when it is broken?
An egg.

ZAÏRE

An animal built a house,
but it lacks a door; it
lacks windows. What is it?
An egg.

AFGHANISTAN

In a bowl of china are fixed
Two liquids with colors unmixed.
An egg.

TANZANIA

My house is large; it
has no door.
An egg.

KENYA

Nyumba yakwa ītarī ndirica kana
mirango.
Itumbī.

———————

My house has neither
windows nor doors.
What is it?
An egg.

IRELAND

"Do you know what?"
"I know his brother!"

SPAIN

Una arquita blanca como la cal;
todos la saben abrir,
y ninguno cerrar.
El huevo.

———————

A small white chest
Quite like lime;
All know how to open it;
Not one knows how to close it.
The egg.

SCOTLAND

Oh ye cannae shove yer grannie
aff the bus,
Oh ye cannae shove yer grannie
aff the bus,
Ye cannae shove yer grannie
For she's yer mammie's
mammie,
Ye cannae shove yer grannie aff
the bus.

BANGLADESH

A tenant went to his landlord to file a complaint.

    Tenant: Sir, why is rain seeping through the ceiling?

    Landlord: The rent is only fourteen *taka*. For that price do you expect sherbet (a fruit drink) to fall?

JAPAN

「お金ほしい。？」
「うん　ちょうだい。」
すると一方の子供がこぶしを振り上げ相手を打つふりをしながら
「はい　ごえ〜ん　」

———————

"Do you want money?"

"Yes. Give me some."

Then a child, lifting his fist and pretending to hit his friend, says:
"Here you are: GO-u-u-EN."

(Note: In Japan, the unit of money is *yen*; "five yen" is said, "go yen." Also, a bell at the temple sounds "GO-u-u-EN" when hit. This particular joke is a prank played on friends.)

U.S.S.R.

БАРБУ

Барбу играл в мяч. Мячик подпрыгнул и разбил стекло.
Перепугался Барбу и спрятался под ковёр, что висел на верёвке.
А тут дедушка вышел — выбивать пыль из ковра.

———————

Barbu

Barbu was playing ball. The ball bounced up and broke the window.

    Barbu got scared and hid under a carpet that was hanging on the clothesline.

And out came Grandfather—to beat the dust out of the carpet.

U.S.A.

Once a pirate made a baloney sandwich, and his parrot said, "Baloney, baloney, baloney." Then a man fell overboard, and the parrot said, "Don't just stand there! Pull him up! Pull him up! Pull him up!" Then the ship hit a big black rock, and the parrot said, "Hit a big black rock! Hit a big black rock! Hit a big black rock!" After that, they started going real fast, and the parrot said, "Going ninety miles an hour! Going ninety miles an hour! Going ninety miles an hour!"

When they came ashore, they all went to church, and the preacher said, "The Lord lives up there." And the parrot said, "Baloney, baloney, baloney!" The preacher shook his finger and said, "The Devil lives down there!" And the parrot said, "Don't just stand there! Pull him up! Pull him up! Pull him up!" At that, the preacher got mad and hit the parrot on the head with a big black book, and the parrot said, "Hit a big black rock! Hit a big black rock! Hit a big black rock!" Of course, they ran out of there real fast, and the parrot said, "Going ninety miles an hour! Going ninety miles an hour! Going ninety miles an hour!" The end.

—Scott Prichard
Second grade
Lubbock, Texas

INDEX

Languages represented

MORE FREE SPIRIT BOOKS